Aug 23, 1980

To Nora I Hope you
enjoy our book

Hy Roth

The Little People

by

Hy Roth and Robert Cromie

Foreword by
Irving Wallace

Dedicated to
Alice Cromie
and
Marilyn Roth

Library of Congress Catalog Card Number: 79-51195

ISBN: 0-89696-024-2

Published simultaneously in Canada by

Beaverbooks, Pickering, Ontario

Manufactured in the United States of America by

Halliday Lithographic

West Hanover, Massachusetts

First Edition

Contents

Photo Credits

Charles King; Ken Young; Charles Schultz; Al Niemic; Mr. and Mrs. Jim MacAtee; Mr. and Mrs. Cliff Krainek (Graphic Antiquity); Mr. and Mrs. Steve Balkin; Dr. Stuart Schneider; Mr. and Mrs. Marvin Kreisman; Bob Hudovernik; Ken Apollo/ Exile Traveling Photographic Gallery; Frank Milligan; Jack Levin; Circus World Museum, Baraboo, Wisconsin, Mr. Bob Parkinson; The Free Library of Philadelphia, Mr. Robert F. Looney; Mr. and Mrs. Ron Becker; America Hurrah Antiques, New York City; The Chicago Historical Society; The Newberry Library, Chicago; The Chicago Public Library; Stan Wanberg; John Lerch; Charlotte Franklin; The Brown Shoe Company, St. Louis, Missouri; The *St. Louis Post-Dispatch,* St. Louis, Missouri; Mr. Bill Veeck; Mr. and Mrs. Ralph Altman; Mickey Pallas; David P. Grath; Joe Cavalier; Janet Clemento; Victor Margolin; Matthews Weber Photos; United Press International; Sandy Brokaw; Arnie Mills and Associates; Ellen Land-Weber; Karin Perkins; John McGuire; Mr. and Mrs. Leon Jacobson; Len Walle; Alice Cromie; *Chicago Tribune,* John Randolph, Jay Dayton.

Foreword

THIS is a wonderful big book about a mad assortment of little people.

The timing of the book seems curiously appropriate. The thrust toward bigness—from buildings to ocean liners—was a feature of the 19th century and early 20th century. Now, in the latter half of the 20th century, we have entered into a time of appreciation for smallness. Indeed, we are part of the Age of Miniaturization. Miniature electronic devices helped us to the moon and to the far reaches of outer space, micro-photography helped us explore the long lost world of nature, microfiche helped us preserve our heritage.

In this latter day appreciation of the diminutive, only one factor has been overlooked. That factor is—the small human beings of the world.

Now, at last, two large-hearted communicators have repaired that omission. With their book, *The Little People,* author Robert Cromie and art director-artist Hy Roth have given the world the definitive work on every major midget in history, past to present day. And in this book, through word and picture, they have done more for little people (and for those of us interested in their peculiar and courageous individual stories) than anyone since Jonathan Swift gave us his Lilliputians in *Gulliver's Travels* and since T. H. White gave the descendants of the Lilliputians in *Mistress Marsham's Revenge.*

Of course, the collaborators who produced this book came to their pleasurable task with the best of credentials. Robert Cromie, an old friend, was a onetime columnist on the *Chicago Tribune,* author of numerous books as well as co-author of *The Great Fire: Chicago, 1871,* and is widely known for his hostmanship on the television shows, *Book Beat* and *The Cromie Circle.* Hy Roth, responsible for the visual side of this book, is highly regarded as a designer, satirical cartoonist, and instructor at Columbia College, Chicago. He is also a collector of midget-related memorabilia.

I need not speak of the contents of this saga—alive with drama and histrionics extolling the virtues of midgetdom—for they will speak for themselves. But I can't resist giving the reader a slight preview of the pleasures awaiting him when he dips into this book. Recently, as a diversion from my novelistic endeavors, I joined my family—wife Sylvia, son David, daughter Amy, writers all—in creating *The Book of Lists.* Because I am still enamoured of lists, I decided the best way I could give the reader a sampling of the delights that live between these covers was by creating a list, to wit:

THE 10 BIGGEST
LITTLE PEOPLE IN HISTORY

1. TOM THUMB—25 inches tall
   The best-known midget in history. He was received by President Abraham Lincoln and Queen Victoria.

2. LAVINIA WARREN BUMP—32 inches tall
   She married Tom Thumb, outlived him, and became a Christian Scientist.

3. GENERAL MITE—18 inches tall
   He is alleged to once have had a love affair with normal-sized, renowned opera singer Adelina Patti.

4. LUCIA ZARATE——20 inches tall
   She was from Mexico and weighed 4.7 pounds.

5. COUNT PRIMO MAGRI—32 inches tall
   Lavinia Bump's second husband. Once arrested for not marrying a normal-sized woman whose favors he had enjoyed.

6. JEFFREY HUDSON—19 inches tall
   In 1649, he fought a pistol duel with a normal-sized opponent and killed him.

7. MONSIEUR RICHEBOURG—21 inches tall
   A spy during the French Revolution, he was dressed in baby's clothes and carried by a nursemaid through enemy lines to deliver information.

8. EDDIE GAEDEL—43 inches tall
   The smallest baseball player ever to come to bat in the major leagues. His strike zone was 1½″ and in his one appearance for the St. Louis Browns he earned a base on balls.

9. CAROLINA CRACHAMI—19 inches tall
   In 1824, she died in London. Her father tried to recover her body, but it had been sold to the College of Surgeons for dissection. Thereafter, her skeleton was put on exhibition.

10. LYA GRAF—21 inches tall
    She became famous in 1933 when she was photographed sitting on tycoon J. P. Morgan's knee during a Congressional committee hearing. She went back to Germany where the Nazis put her to death in Auschwitz.

There is so much more about these people—and hundreds of others—in the pages of this book. I suggest the reader step inside Lilliput for the time of his (or her) life.

IRVING WALLACE

Prince Dennison. (Credit Circus World Museum, Baraboo, Wis.)

Introduction

BEINGS who are far smaller than usual have always held an intense fascination for persons of more normal dimension, as any survey of the world's mythology or folklore demonstrates.

This is true whether the little people are flesh-and-blood, such as the fiery Jeffrey Hudson or wistful Carolina Crachami, or fanciful: Ireland's leprechauns, Scotland's dread Black Dwarf, the oft-helpful earthmen of Switzerland, the mine dwarfs of England or Europe, or the mountain dwarfs of Germanic and Scandinavian legend.

Leprechauns were—some would say are—mischievous but not basically nasty. If you came on one while he worked as a cobbler (his only trade) and managed to seize him, you might, if you were very careful, frighten him into disclosing where the treasure leprechauns always possessed was hidden. But if he could somehow trick you into taking your eyes off him for even the most fleeting of moments, he would vanish.

The mine dwarfs of Cornwall and other parts of England, if spied upon by human miners or not given food, could cause a roof to come down, firedamp to ignite, tools to break, or water to seep into the tunnels. If placated with gifts, however, these tiny creatures would often warn of imminent danger by rapping, a service which won them the name of "Knockers" in the British Isles.

The Black Dwarf, whose character undoubtedly gave Sir Walter Scott the idea for his novel of that name, is described in *Brewer's Dictionary of Phrase and Fable* as a "gnome of the most malignant character." Border dwellers held that he was responsible for every evil that befell their field animals.

Another diminutive but extremely unpleasant fellow was Alberich, ruler of the Scandinavian dwarfs, who was in charge of the treasure owned by King Nibelung, whom you will recall from Wagner's *Das Rheingold.*

In early Teutonic tales the dwarfs, who lived underground for the most part, were guardians of precious metals and famed for their skill in making swords or jeweled rings with magical powers. Many dwarfs were very rich and could predict the future. Some were open-handed with humans they liked, yet extremely vindictive to those who crossed them. They were not above stealing crops, or even children, but anyone robbing them found very bad luck in the future or discovered, on reaching home with the booty, that his pilfered treasure had turned into withered leaves along the way.

According to Teutonic myth, the gods created dwarfs from grubs found in the decaying body of Ymir, father of all the giants, who was killed by Odin, a giant and a god. These dwarfs are credited with mixing the potion called hydromel, also known as "the mead of the poets" because anyone quaffing it became both an instant poet and extremely wise. Dwarf artisans made Odin's spear, Gungnir, which always pierced what it was thrown at, and Mjollnir, Thor's magic hammer, which always returned to his hand after the god of thunder hurled it at someone.

Sometimes they made less lethal things: the hair of gold for Sif, Thor's wife, which grew as if it were real; the golden boar which drew Frey's chariot, and his marvel-ous ship, *Skidbladnir,* which could outsail anything on the oceans yet be carried in his pocket when not in use.

It was the dwarfs, too, who devised a method of restraining the wolf, Fenrir, an implacable enemy of the gods, after the gods themselves had failed to find anything strong enough to hold him. The dwarfs, as *The New Larousse Encyclopedia of Mythology* tells us, made a chain out of "the miaul of a cat, a beard of a woman, the roots of the mountain, the tendons of a bear, the breath of a fish and the spittle of a bird." Fenrir finally tore his way loose and killed Odin, but that is another story.

Trolls, incidentally, another sort of dwarf found in Scandinavia, lived in hills or under the earth, and were understandably upset by excessive noise, since Thor frequently sailed his hammer at them, keeping the trolls, presumably, on a kind of surly alert.

Then there were elves, more attractive than any human, who loved to dance by

Mike (or Ike?) Matina of Singer's Lilliputians.

moonlight (you could see their tiny footprints in the morning dew). Many an unwary traveler, joining their frolics after being overcome by the beauty of some female elf, was never seen again, or was found dead when daylight came.

Other minuscule supernatural beings include the Germanic kobolds, who looked human, except for their very small stature, and always wore pointed hoods. Kobolds preferred to live in cellars, barns or other outbuildings, and happily performed such tasks as cutting wood, carrying water, currying the horses, or feeding cattle. The kobold brought luck to the household that treated him properly, which meant supplying a few table scraps and some milk. But if this were not done, accidents happened to servant or *hausfrau:* broken dishes, hands scalded, tables overturned.

"When such mishaps occurred," the *Larousse* reports, "she would hear in the corner the malicious chuckle of the kobold."

Top left: Christopher and Edwin Sparling with unknown friend; center, Maggie Minot of Belle Plaine, La. (Eisenmann Photo.) At right, Major Ong in San Francisco studio; bottom left, Miss Rebecca Invers, Marmont City, Ind. At center, Anton Roubal, as he looked in 1880 (Photo by A. L. Jones, Chicago.) At right is Princess Winnie Wee, star attraction at Coney Island's Dreamland.

Perhaps the strangest spirit of all was the leshy, which could be found in Slavic forests. The leshy had cheeks of a bluish cast, green eyes, and wore his shoes on the wrong foot. He also possessed the useful trait of towering treetop tall when in the woods and dwindling to such tiny size in the open that he could hide under a leaf. He cast no shadow.

If a leshy ever finds you lost in the forest, however, do not be alarmed. They are normally without malice, though it *might* be wise to put your clothes on backward and switch shoes, a tribute which disarms the leshy completely.

The kobolds had their equivalent in the brownies of northern England and Scotland. The brownies did housework at night, would summon the midwife when needed, caused swarming bees to settle (at least in Cornwall), and also took umbrage if bread and milk or cream were not left for them. But the one sure way to get rid of a brownie was to make him a suit of clothes. Angered, he would put it on and leave for good.

The Eskimos had a god called Eeyeekalduk, a small, dark-faced, manlike creature, largely friendly; but Brazilian Indians feared Kurupira, a protector of game and hater of humans, while in Egypt there was a god called Bes, a fat and pugnacious dwarf, fond of dancing. Bes presided over childbearing, and his statue could protect a family from scorpions, snakes, crocodiles, and other dangerous intruders.

The sometimes alarming *Larousse* warns:

> To this day, it would seem, the monumental southern gate of Karnak serves as a dwelling-place for a knock-kneed dwarf, whose gross head is embellished with a formidable beard. Woe to the stranger who coming across him in the dusk of evening, laughs at his grotesque figure! For the monster will leap at his throat and strangle him. He is the Bes of ancient Egypt ... not yet resigned to abandoning altogether the scenes which once witnessed his greatness.

Nor should it be forgotten that Vishnu, one of the Hindu Trinity, returned in his fifth avatar (incarnation) as Vamana, a dwarf. Vishnu, in fact, is reported to have once appeared as so diminutive a dwarf that he imagined the water-filled footprint of a cow to be a lake.

But enough of myth and legend. Now that the stage is set, let us talk about real little people, concerning whom it is our wish to offer an entertaining and instructive book, with many prints and photographs—but not a *sensational* book.

We would like it to be understood at the outset that little people are little only in *stature,* because of some failure of bodily function. Their misfortune it is to be seen as if forever viewed through a minifying glass. Otherwise they are like everyone else: merry or sad, intelligent or dull, gregarious or withdrawn, thoughtful or happy-go-lucky.

Terri Schultz, a *Chicago Tribune* reporter, covered a convention of the Little People of America a few years ago, and summed up, in a few sentences, both the attitude of many members of the general public and the sense of personal dignity that the little people now possess.

> The clubwomen meant well. With giggles and smiles, with their perfumes gently engulfing the hotel hallway, they bent towards the carpeting and chirped . . . : "Hello, little people."
> And the dwarfs obligingly lifted the corners of their mouths in what passed for smiles.
>
> They had heard it all before. The elevator conversation. "How's the weather down there?" "How did you get that way?" "Hi, shorty." Or the child whispering: "What's that?" And the mother admonishing, "Just be grateful you're not that way."
> Most dwarfs successfully ignore the blows to their psyches. They don't have to make people laugh any more to earn a living. . . .

Unidentified comics (British carte de visite.)

The point is well made. Weary, naturally enough, of being regarded as freaks, capable of making a livelihood only by exhibiting themselves in dime museums, traveling shows, or carnivals, today's little people are working in a variety of jobs, performing them every bit as well as their larger associates, and trying, with great success, to "Think Big." That is the motto of the Little People of America, a group formed in 1957 by Billy Barty, the Hollywood actor.

In a society that has become more enlightened, at least in this regard, the parents of children who will never reach normal size now rarely hide them away. Instead the relatives also join the LPA as auxiliary members, and do what they can to ensure as ordinary a life as possible for those who find themselves in a world built on too grand a scale.

A comparative handful of little people still perform as circus clowns—an honorable and respected profession. But there also are, among LPA members, schoolteachers, secretaries, writers, clerks, draftsmen, TV repairmen, bankers, business executives, construction workers, artists, tavern owners, engineers, and at least two who drive cross-country rigs, huge truck and trailer outfits equipped, as are many little people's cars, with extension pedals. There also has been a twenty-eight-inch nightclub bouncer in Columbus, Ohio, said to be remarkably effective in quieting noisy patrons who turn to see who is tugging at their coattails. Immediate sobriety resulted. And there is a publicity director for a major league baseball team.

More than half a century ago Walter de la Mare wrote a novel called *Memoirs of a Midget.* In a foreword to the Reader's Club edition of that excellent book, Carl Van Doren wrote of Miss M., the charming heroine:

How far Miss M. is true to life, only other midgets can say, and they do not all agree. There is no sign that the glands which have made her smaller than other people have made her otherwise different from them. She is merely a woman in miniature. If she lacked sight or hearing or speech, feet or hands, or were distorted or disfigured, almost anybody would know how to make allowances for her. As a midget she is handicapped not in herself but in relation to her world, her history is a history of all the handicapped. And her wish is the deepest wish of all of them: "that one friend at any rate," she ends, "will consent in his love and wisdom to take me seriously, and to remember me, not with scorn or even with pity, but as if, life for life, we shared the world on equal terms." Here in her is the basic human desire: to be a person among persons.

The Latin poet Lucan also had a thoughtful reminder for us some 1,900 years ago that the disadvantages of smallness are not insurmountable when he wrote: "Pigmies placed on the shoulders of giants see more than the giants themselves."

Cover of Yellow Dwarf series, 19th-century paperbacks.

Suma Smaun, entertainer and acrobat of the 1880's.

Singer's Midgets on stage.

*Col. Gary Storching,
"Championship
Skater of
Connecticut."*

Early History

NY HISTORY OF THE LIT-
tle people of ancient times is for the most
part impossible to set down in detail or
with any degree of accuracy. For some only
their names remain. For others it is uncertain whether they were true dwarfs or simply somewhat below average height.

For example, was Attila the Hun a
dwarf, as the English historian Edward
Gibbon indicates? Gibbon's description of
Attila, or Etzel as he was known in early
Germanic writings, comes from Priscus of
Panium, who visited Attila's camp in A.D.
449 with a Roman mission. Priscus found
"the Scourge of God," as Attila was called
after conquering much of western Europe,
to be of squat build, with a large head, flat
nose, and thin beard. But was he a dwarf?

Equally ambiguous is the biblical portrayal of Zacchaeus in Luke 19:

And Jesus entered and passed through
Jericho.

And, behold, there was a man named
Zacchaeus, which was the chief among the
publicans, and he was rich.

And he sought to see Jesus who he was;
and could not for the press, because he was
little of stature.

And he ran before, and climbed up into
a sycamore tree to see him: for he was to
pass that way.

And when Jesus came to the place, he
looked up, and saw him, and said unto
him, Zacchaeus, make haste, and come
down; for today I must abide at thy house.

And he made haste, and came down,
and received him joyfully.

It seems *probable* that Zacchaeus was
small enough to have qualified as a dwarf
(4 feet 10 inches is the accepted dividing
line), since men and women were shorter

in those days. But this, too, is guesswork.

Aesop, according to some accounts, was a dwarf. A former slave, he was thrown over a cliff at Delphi by priests enraged at his "blasphemies," according to legend. He lived in the sixth century B.C. Chambers' *Biographical Dictionary*, however, adds: "The tradition of his ugliness and his buffoonery may be dismissed." So?

Pepin the Short, son of Charles Martel and father of the Emperor Charlemagne, was, as you will have guessed, not tall. But *how* short he was is anyone's guess. Pepin, King of the Franks, lived from 715 to 768.

Ladislas I, King of Poland, born in 1260 or 1261, bore the nickname Lokietek, which means "the Spanhigh." It seems safe to assume he was dwarf-size, since a span equals nine inches. In any event, Ladislas, before he died in 1333, took measures which led to a strong and united Polish monarchy and was crowned at Cracow in 1320 with the blessing of Pope John XXII.

Many other famous persons, now centuries dead and forever safe from measurement, also are said to have been dwarfs. Among them were Nebuchadrezzar, King of Babylon; Croesus, King of Lydia, the man with the golden touch; Charles III, who ruled Sicily and Naples in the fourteenth century, and Bertoldo, peasant-born adviser to Alboin, King of the Lombards, some 1,400 years ago, of whom a delightful and probably apocryphal story is told.

Bertoldo supposedly angered the Queen to such an extent that he was ordered to be hanged. The doomed man begged a final favor, which Alboin granted: that he be permitted to choose the tree on which he would die. Bertoldo and the hangman then set out, only to return hours later. The executioner explained that although they had inspected innumerable trees, none suited the finicky Bertoldo. Alboin, obviously glad of a chance to relent, then pardoned Bertoldo.

One of the earliest of the little people whose name is known was Khnumhotpu or Knoumtoptuwo, who served as linen steward to an Egyptian monarch some 2,500 years before Christ. His statue shows him to have been well below average height.

It is recorded also that the first Spanish explorer to see the court of Montezuma found dwarfs among that ruler's attendants, and there is a story that Philetas of Cos, a poet and grammarian who lived about 330 B.C., was so diminutive that he wore shoes weighted with lead to avoid being blown away on windy days. Philetas was tutor to Ptolemy Philadelphus.

The Ptolemies of early Egypt brought members of the Akka pygmy tribe from Equatorial Africa back to their courts, and Homer, in *The Iliad*, added to the mystery and the misinformation about pygmies when he wrote:

> When under the order of their chiefs they had arranged themselves in battle array, the Trojans advanced noisily like a cloud of birds, making their loud cries heard. So raises itself to heaven the outcry of storks when they flee from winter and the continual rains. They utter shrill cries, they fly over the ocean, they bear carnage and death to the men called pygmies; and from high in the air they give them dreadful combat.

Pliny supports this insupportable yarn, claiming of the pygmies, whose height he underestimates at about 27 inches:

> It is said that, borne upon the backs of rams and of goats and armed with arrows, they descend all together at springtime to the seacoast, and eat the eggs and the little ones of these birds; that this expedition lasts three months; that otherwise they could not resist the increasing multitudes of the storks. . . .

It is certain that dwarfs not only were known in all parts of the world hundreds of years ago, but were coveted by kings and members of the upper classes as servants, jesters, conversation pieces, or pets, perhaps on a par with a favorite dog or cat.

Many of the early Roman emperors kept dwarfs. Tiberius is said to have permitted his favorite to sit at table with him and speak freely, even on matters of state. Domitian ordered a troupe of dwarf gladiators trained to take part in the circus spectacles. Augustus, Alexander Severus, and the infamous Heliogabalus also owned dwarfs or midgets.

Julia, the niece of Augustus, had two little people whose names we know: Conopas, and a former slave girl, Andromeda, each 28 inches tall. Marc Antony, who fell for the charms of Cleopatra, is mentioned as having a dwarf called Sisyphus, not to be confused with the legendary rock-and-roll man.

There even were two Roman knights, Marius Maximus and Marcus Tullius, who are known to have been dwarflike because of the dimensions of their mummified bodies.

So much in demand were dwarfs that the Romans used to create them artificially. *Nanus* was the word for a natural dwarf and *pumilo* for one made by starving small children or stunting their growth by confining them in some manner. It is difficult to believe that one of the more exotic dwarfing recipes was truly effective: anointing the backbone with ointment made from bats, moles, and dormice.

There even is one story that a Chinese dwarf was formed in the shape of a large vase in which he was kept during much of his childhood, a story one should hate to see authenticated.

The *Enciclopedia dello Spettacolo*, published in Rome in 1958, lists among early little people a Milanese dwarf of the sixteenth century who could be fitted without effort into a parrot's cage; and in the eighteenth century the Persian Dwarf, who

sang, danced, and could speak eight languages. Also Il Piccolo Arlecchino (the Little Harlequin), who was an admirer of C. Bertinazzi, a celebrated clown known as Carlino. Il Piccolo Arlecchino was about 30 inches tall.

Surely one of the most thoughtful of all the dwarf-collectors was Isabelle d'Este, who added a wing to her *palazzo* to house her dwarfs and even remembered a couple of them in her will.

C. J. S. Thompson, in his *The Mystery and Lore of Monsters* (London, 1930), cites a number of things which indicate how much attention was paid to dwarfs by the European rulers and noble families:

Charles IX of France, whose mother was Catherine de' Medici, not only gathered dwarfs from various other lands but in 1572 was presented with three by the Emperor of Germany. Catherine herself also liked dwarfs and at one time had five: Majowski, given her by Charles; Merlin, Mandricart, Pelavine, and Rodomont.

Thompson also mentions the banquet given in 1566 by Cardinal Vitelli of Italy, at which the guests were served by thirty-four tiny waiters.

Perhaps the earliest mention of an English dwarf is found in an old ballad which begins: "In Arthur's Court Tom Thumb did live." If there really was a King Arthur, and if he did have a dwarf at his court, this surely would make Tom Thumb (whose name was later borrowed by P. T. Barnum for perhaps the most famous dwarf of all time) the first known English dwarf. But there are difficulties:

It is hard to accept as genuine someone no larger than his ploughman father's thumb, especially since the ballad describes Tom's being swallowed by a cow and a giant, riding in the ear of a horse, hiding in the holes in Swiss cheese, darting through a keyhole to escape a hungry rat, being swallowed by a fish and saved by a cook in the royal kitchen, and finally being fatally gobbled up by a spider!

Of authentic English dwarfs, the first to find a home at court was John Jarvis, only two feet tall, who was page for Queen Mary I. Edward VI, Mary's brother, also had a dwarf on the royal roster, of whom virtually nothing is known but his curious name, Xit. A great deal is known, however, about Jeffrey Hudson, whom you will meet in more detail later. He served Henrietta Maria, Queen of Charles I.

Henry VIII had as jester Will Sommers, a dwarf who was so popular a figure that a contemporary poet wrote of him:

And stoop he did too; yet in all the court,
Few men were more belov'd than was this fool.

There is mention in the accounts of Henry VIII of monies spent to make garments for "our court fool." And an indication of the regard the King must have had for his little jester is that when Henry was on his deathbed, he restored, at Will's request, part of the lands confiscated from Sommers' former master.

Another extremely well known "fool" (and the word meant simply "jester," although some court fools were indeed simple-minded) was Archibald Armstrong, who served both James I and his son, Charles I of England. Hudson, incidentally, was in the Queen's service while Armstrong was with Charles I, as were a very talented little painter, Richard Gibson, and his wife, Anne Shepherd, each about 3 feet 10 inches high.

Robert Ker Porter, an English painter who traveled widely and was in the British diplomatic service, mentions in his *Travels in Russia and Sweden* having seen numerous dwarfs in Russia. Those in the service of noblemen, he declared: ". . . stand for hours behind their lord's chair, holding his snuff box or awaiting his commands. . . . These little beings are generally the gayest dressed persons in the service of their lord and are attired in a uniform or livery of very costly materials. . . ."

Peter the Great, the Russian Czar, celebrated the marriage of his niece, Princess Anne, by staging a wedding two days later between his own favorite dwarf, Valakoff, and a female dwarf owned by a princess. Peter had invitations to the affair delivered by dwarfs "richly clad," and the guests included seventy-two dwarfs, most of them from the Czar's household. Peter himself held the crown above the bride's head. This was in 1710.

A GREAT CURIOSITY !
MISS MINNIE OBOM !
ASSUREDLY THE
**SMALLEST LADY KNOWN
TO EXIST IN THE WORLD !**
SHE IS
13 Years of Age !
25 Inches High !
And weighs
ONLY 10 POUNDS !

This little lady weighed only two and three quarters pounds, at her birth, and grew to her present size at her eighth year. She is remarkably handsome, bright, and perfect in form and feature.

No little lady ever exhibited, can at all compare with her, either in beauty or intelligence.

General Shade, whose professional career began about 1860 (Photo by Robbins, Huntington, Id., c. 1870.)

Fairs, Circuses, Dime Museums, and Carnivals

ASIDE FROM BEING A CU-riosity for some wealthy patron there were few occupations open to the little people of earlier days. By the late sixteenth century many were forced to exhibit themselves to a fascinated but often mocking public to earn enough to survive.

There were various ways to do this. Sometimes one found a manager, who would handle one or two dwarfs or midgets and exhibit them on request for a small fee. The showman would travel with his tiny troupe from place to place, often carrying his miniature attractions in a box. Inns, taverns, or coffeehouses also were popular spots for such displays.

An easier way, especially for those little people who possessed some skill at singing, dancing, or other types of entertainment, or happened to be extraordinarily small in size, was to appear at fairs, and much later at circuses, carnivals, or dime museums.

Here the patrons sought out the "freaks," as out-of-the-ordinary persons used to be called. The thoughtless term also included giants, very fat or very thin men and women, or those with malformed bodies or the ability to twist or contort themselves in bizarre fashion. Exotic or unnatural animals also were displayed.

One of the earlier instances of a dwarf being exhibited for money is found in *Chronicles of England* by John Stow, a tailor who in his late years became interested in writing and antiquarian pursuits. Stow, who lived from 1525 to 1605, mentions having seen in 1581 "two Dutchmen of strange statures." One was "a giant," who would even draw attention today, at 7 feet 7 inches. The other was a 3-foot dwarf.

They were a pitiful pair. The giant was lame. He had broken both legs lifting a loaded beer barrel. The dwarf also was lame, seemingly from birth, since he had

Wybrand Lolkes and wife. (18th century engraving.)

only stumps for arms. But he danced and performed other tricks and, Stow adds, could walk upright between the giant's legs, and the feather in his hat touched nothing.

The two were in London when Stow saw them, perhaps at St. Bartholomew's Fair, which was held at Smithfield from the mid-twelfth century until it was ordered closed as a public nuisance in 1855.

Colin Clair, in his excellent book *Human Curiosities* (London and New York, 1968), mentions a dwarf, John Ducker (or Decker) who was on exhibition in 1610. A physician named Platter wrote:

> . . . I saw John Ducker, an Englishman, whom some of his own countrymen carried up and down to get money by sight of him. I have his picture by me, drawn at full length; he was about forty-five years of age, as far as might be discerned by his face . . . he was only two and a half feet high. . . . A less than he I have never seen.

Clair's book is crowded with contemporary descriptions of dwarfs and giants exhibited at the various fairs and other places in London during the sixteenth, seventeenth, and eighteenth centuries. Some were deformed as well as small. And some became famous, such as John Wormbergh, the Swiss dwarf, who was only 31 inches high at the age of thirty-seven. He was drowned in 1695 when a box in which a porter was carrying him over a gangplank fell into the water at Rotterdam. The porter swam ashore.

St. Bartholomew's Fair had been in existence more than five hundred years by the time the forty-four-year-old Wormbergh died, and it is probable he had appeared there. The fair began in 1133 under the auspices of Rahere, a former court jester turned monk. Rahere was granted a charter by Henry I to found the Priory of St. Bartholomew in 1123, and permission to start the fair followed. Smithfield, a marshland, had been an execution site for condemned criminals.

Owen Farrell. (Chicago Historical Society Coll.)

Rahere originally was allowed to hold a three-day fair (before, on, and after St. Bartholomew's Day). Later, to ensure better weather, the fair was open at the end of August and extended to ten days. It seems to have been remarkably like the traveling carnivals later seen in great numbers in the United States. There were pickpockets, "freak" shows, gamblers, cheats, food sellers, gypsies, and a gullible public.

A new attraction was added in 1305 when the ban against executions at Smithfield during the fair was lifted and thousands of patrons witnessed a legal killing.

Among the early little people seen at St. Bartholomew's Fair was Wybrand Lolkes, a native of West Friesland, who was 27 inches tall. He learned to be a watchmaker and jeweler from an artisan in Amsterdam, then moved to Rotterdam and opened his own shop. Business was bad, and he and his wife, who was of normal stature, finally came to London in 1790 after appearing at a few Dutch fairs. The couple had three children, also of normal size. Lolkes, who was described as very strong but "of a morose temper," returned to Holland after one season. At the age of sixty, he still weighed only 57 pounds.

Another Hollander, Simon Paap, born in 1789, also is said to have been displayed at St. Bartholomew's. Contemporary reports say he drew crowds of 20,000 on some of his appearances while touring England, perhaps because he dressed in a spectacular Dutch costume of blue and white, with gold buttons on the jacket. Paap, only an inch taller than Lolkes, liked to drink wine, take snuff, and smoke a pipe, but did none to excess. Sometimes he dressed like a small child while walking the streets of London, to avoid unwelcome attention. Paap was presented to the Queen and the Royal Family in 1815, and returned to Holland sometime after 1818. He died in 1828, aged thirty-nine.

Owen Farrell, the Irish Dwarf, was among the many little people seen at the same fair, although about a century earlier

Rickett's Circus, Philadelphia, 1793. (Chicago Public Library Coll.)

than Paap. Farrell, so strong he is said to have been able to carry two men on each arm, never made a consistent living from his exhibitions, perhaps because he was 45 inches in height. Eventually he became a beggar in London. Finally, desperate for funds, he sold his body—for future delivery—to a certain Dr. Omrod. When the Irish Dwarf's unhappy life inded in 1742, his skeleton wound up on display at Glasgow University.

One of the eighteenth century's most renowned dwarfs was Matthew Buchinger (or Buckinger), a misshapen little German, born in Anspach in 1674. He had no feet, legs, or thighs, and only stumps in place of hands. He was 29 inches high. Buchinger came to England during the reign of George I, and found as patron Robert Harley, the Earl of Oxford. Buchinger, ignoring his many handicaps, was a competent sketch artist, wrote in a beautifully flowing style, played several musical instruments, and could even load and fire a pistol.

Despite his grotesque appearance, Buchinger is said to have had "a handsome face." Even this hardly explains how he could have found four normal-size women to marry him, with whom he fathered eleven children. One melancholy account describes an incident involving his second wife, "a very perverse woman," who not only spent most of his money on clothes and fine living but used to beat him regularly. Once, however, she made the mistake of doing so with others present. This "so provoked him that he flew at her with such force, that he threw her down and getting upon her so beat her with his stumps that he almost killed her."

So great an impression did Buchinger make on his era that after his death in 1732(?) a Dublin poet wrote an elegy that began:

C. A. Brandenburgh's Dime Museum, Philadelphia Pa., in late 19th century. (Free Library of Philadelphia Coll.) Inset Sarah E. Belton, as she appeared at Brandenburgh's.

Poor Buchinger at last is dead and gone,
A lifeless trunk who was a living one;
Trunk, did I say, wherein all virtues met?
I should have call'd him a rich cabinet.

E. V. Lucas, in his *A Wanderer in London* (London, 1907), had this to say about St. Bartholomew's Fair, half a century after it had closed for good:

I passed into Smithfield's large vacancy, where Bartholomew Fair—which was in its serious side a fair for cloth—used to be held every Bartholomew's Day until 1855, when the law stepped in and said No. The pleasure portion was the most extraordinary chaos of catchpenny booths, theatricals, *ferae naturae*, wild beasts, cheap jacks and charlatans that England has ever seen.

Charles Dickens, the English novelist, in his *Sketches by "Boz"* (London, 1836), tells of Greenwich Fair, of which "in our earlier years, we were a constant frequenter." Of particular interest is this passage:

The dwarfs are also objects of great curiosity, and as a dwarf, a giantess, a living skeleton, a wild Indian, "a young lady of singular beauty, with perfectly white hair and pink eyes," and two or three other natural curiosities, are usually exhibited together for the small charge of a penny, they attract very numerous audiences. The best thing about a dwarf is, that he had always a little box, about two feet six inches high, into which, by long practice, he can just manage to get, by doubling himself up like a boot-jack; this box is painted outside like a six-roomed house, and as the crowd see him ring a bell, or fire a pistol out of the first-floor window, they verily believe that it is his ordinary town residence, divided like other mansions into drawing-rooms, dining-parlours, and bedchambers. Shut up in this case, the unfortunate little object is brought out to delight the throng by holding a facetious dialogue with the proprietor: in the course of which, the dwarf (who is always particularly drunk) pledges himself to sing a comic song inside, and pays

The Philadelphia Circus (formerly the National Theatre) which opened in 1876.

various compliments to the ladies, which induce them to "come for'erd" with great alacrity. . . .

The roster of little people who have made their marks in the entertainment world is too long to list completely, even if a list were available. In the nineteenth century, perhaps the busiest time of all for those in show business, there were such as Signor Hervio Nano, who appeared at London's Olympia Theatre in 1843, and the Australian Mary Jane Youngman, known as the dwarf-giantess because of her curious measurements. She was 35 inches high, 42 inches around the shoulders, 51 around the waist, and had legs 2 feet in circumference. Another noted pair was called the Aztec Dwarfs.

The *American Journal of Medical Sciences* (Boston, 1851) carried an account of the two, written by Dr. Mason Warren. He examined them and determined that the boy, who weighed 20½ pounds and was almost 34 inches tall, was seven or eight years old. The girl, 17 pounds and 29½ inches, was about 5 years old. After a long medical description of their skin (dark with a yellowish cast) and their features, including a protruding upper jaw, Dr. Warren adds: "The position generally assumed by these children is peculiar, and may well be compared to that of some of the Simian tribe . . . the boy has a swinging gait, not unlike that of a person slightly intoxicated."

At no point does the doctor question the morality of exhibiting two seemingly backward youngsters who sound in desperate need of help. But he makes this callous observation:

A question naturally arises to an observer first visiting these beings, whether they belong to the human species; and it is only after he becomes accustomed to their appearance that the brotherhood is acknowledged . . . they are without any language of their own. They seem to acquire words rapidly and since their sojourn in Boston have learned to repeat a number such as "Papa," "Mamma," "Ellen," "Take care," etc. . . . with regard to any communication by signs with each other or language which they may have with each other, it appears to be at present not much greater than what might be expected from two intelligent individuals of the canine race.

The *Encyclopaedia Britannica* gives us a brief glimpse of their subsequent history: They appeared in London in 1853—still on exhibition—and were married there fourteen years later. Whether they ever learned to talk properly, or whether they were, as seems possible, brother and sister, is not stated. The supposition first made that they came from an Indian tribe in Central America is contradicted by other statements that they were American Negroes.

Whatever and whoever, their story is a depressing one.

There were many other little people who made a living, and sometimes a good one, in show business in the nineteenth century.

Most likely, the first European circus to visit the United States was directed by a Mr. Faulks and opened in Center Square, Philadelphia, in 1771. This was only three years after Philip Astley, an English trick rider, began the first modern circus in London, near Westminster Bridge. Astley is credited with the discovery that galloping in a circle while standing on horseback enlisted the aid of centrifugal force to keep the horseman upright.

Circuses proliferated rapidly, especially since the fairs began dying out, partly because of pressure from theater owners and in part because of increased rowdyism and violence. By 1793 the first American circus opened in New York and Philadelphia under the ownership of John William Ricketts. In the same year his circus was advertised in Baltimore, and, it was promised, "Mr. Ricketts will this evening perform a great feat of horsemanship. He will leap through a hoop suspended in the air 12 feet high, and recover his situation, the horse being the same speed."

Obviously Astley's discovery had crossed the Atlantic.

Frank Wood, who stood under four feet tall, appeared with Dr. J. I. Lighthall's traveling sideshow that toured the United States, selling patent medicine in the 1870's.

The Polander Dwarf, also known as the Warsaw Wonder, may have been the first little person to appear in a circus in the United States. He rode through a flaming hoop with the Ricketts Circus as early as October 17, 1795.

Another of the early performers was a "Mr. Richards," described simply as "a small person," who danced with the Lafayette Circus somewhere on Canal Street in New York City in 1825.

Calvin Phillips, born in Bridgewater, Connecticut, in 1791, also was entertaining while the nineteenth century and Phillips both were young. He was slightly over 24 inches tall and weighed, it is said, only 11 pounds. He performed in New York in 1810, but details are unavailable, and he died, apparently senile, two years later.

Circuses, carnivals, the dime museums, which sprang up in 1784, vaudeville, the stage, and of course, eventually, the motion pictures were the principal employment opportunities for the little people until comparatively recent times.

Performers were known, usually, not by their own names, but by such exotic ones as Admiral Dot, Major Stevens (he was 48 inches high when P. T. Barnum hired him and was out of the business after Tom Thumb showed up), the Eldorado Dwarf (an uncle of Major Atom), Princess Winnie Wee, Baron Littlefinger, Count Rosebud, the Little Esquimaux Lady, Princess Tiny, Little Lord Robert, Princess Wee Wee, who became the wife of Hop the Frog Man, Lady Little, Commodore Foote, Mrs. Short, Anita the Doll Lady, Wee

Willie Archie, Jennie Quigley the Scottish Queen, often billed as the world's smallest woman, the Little Russian, Prince Nicolai, who was said to have been born in a Siberian prison camp where his father, a disgraced Russian officer, was slaving in the mines, and of course General Tom Thumb, whose marriage to Lavinia Warren Bump was produced and directed by the great Barnum himself and was attended by notables, including Major General Ambrose L. Burnside.

Charles Wilson Peale founded the first dime museum in the United States in Philadelphia in 1784, and the idea spread quickly. Indoor circuses and combination theaters and exhibition halls also sprang up. The Walnut Street Theater, which opened in Philadelphia in 1809, had an indoor arena for equestrian acts. Another showplace in town was the Arch Street Theater, opened in 1829.

The dime museums gave work to very big or very little people, and also displayed strange animals, curious mechanical devices, and even fakes, such as Barnum's mermaid, or Joice Heth, the black woman, who supposedly was 161 years old and had been the nurse of George Washington.

Among the finest of the museums was the Egyptian Hall, in London, where Barnum was to exhibit Tom Thumb, as well as in his own American Museum in New York, which was always gay with waving banners and enormous illustrations of the wonders within. There were also the Boston Museum, Crosby's in Chicago, and away across the country, Dr. Gordon's Museum in San Francisco, where the greatest attraction was the supposed head of Joachim Murieta, a legendary Mexican bandit and folk hero who may or may not have actually lived. Philadelphia had Brandenburgh's Museum, where a little person, Sarah E. Belton, was a star and where women's basketball was played.

One of Barnum's principal competitors was Ezra Stephens, a showman from New England, who started a museum in New York and whose main attractions were Waino and Plutano, the Wild Men of Borneo.

It should come as no surprise to anyone familiar with nineteenth-century promoters that Waino and Plutano, who were captured only after a fierce struggle with four sailors from a ship anchored off the Borneo coast, actually were Hiram and Barney Davis of Waltham, Massachusetts, born in 1825 and 1817 respectively.

It seems doubtful that they could, as advertised, subdue wild tigers. But it does seem a fact that the two little brothers, although either subnormal mentally or sadly uneducated, were abnormally strong. Either could lift a 6-foot man without trouble.

Stephens, known as the Barnum of Maine, displayed the pair against a backdrop representing the jungles of Borneo. Stephens, like the flamboyant Barnum, was a master con artist. Nor were Waino and Plutano his only deceptions. His "dancing turkeys" hopped up and down because he exhibited them on a heated metal platform, and his South American cockatoo was an ordinary American hen, brightly dyed and adorned with extra feathers.

Stephens also showed a third little person, Major Robert Harner, who at eighteen was 40 inches high and weighed 48 pounds, about three more than the brothers from Waltham-Borneo.

Another drawing card of the era was Miss Olaf Krarer, the Little Esquimaux Lady, who—according to a message hand-

Dime museum ticket.

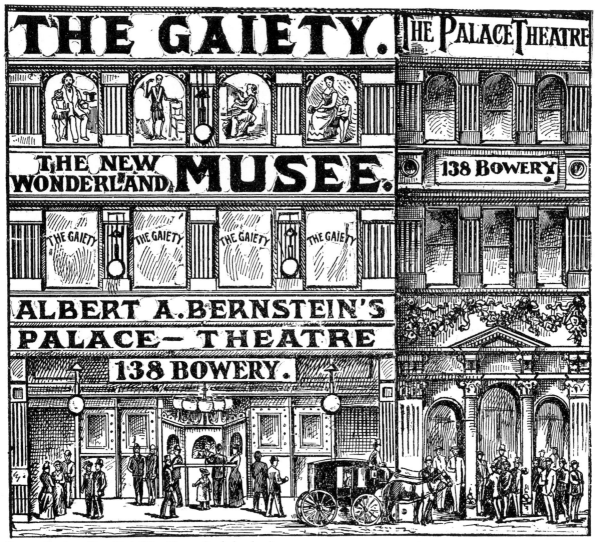

Bowery theatres, New York City. (from 1890's brochure)

written on the back of a photograph of her, probably taken late in the century—was educated, and once lectured at a Minnesota college. Miss Krarer, who usually posed with a dog of diminutive size, always wore her native costume.

One of the few remaining memories of the old dime museums, which began to dwindle in number as the twentieth century drew near, can be found in the *cartes de visite,* the small cards bearing the likenesses of little people, giants, fat ladies, and the inevitable thin man, sold by the thousands to museum customers and often autographed by General Tom Thumb, or Che-Mah, or others of the unusual persons the public paid to see.

One of the world's smallest men, dressed in mandarin robes, rests in Crown Hill Cemetery at Knox, Indiana. The name of the tombstone, which he himself bought, is Che-Mah. He was a native of Chusan and came to the United States in 1881 to join the P. T. Barnum troupe.

Che-Mah, a bright and friendly man, refused to think of himself as anything but normal, according to the people of Knox, and once tried to leave show business for farming. He bought property near town and made a valiant effort, but his Knox neighbors said it took him hours to harness a single horse, and all day for a team. He returned to the circus.

Nothing annoyed Che-Mah more than

Pearson's Midgets, featuring Major Tiny and wife. Traveling sideshow, 1920's.

Snapshots of neighborhood sideshow being set up in Chicago, early 20th century.

to be teased about his size. When this happened he would touch his head and say: "The mind, not the body, measures the man."

He was twice married to women of normal size, and had a son by his first wife, a trapeze performer, Louisa Coleman, from whom he was divorced later. When he was sixty-two, he quit traveling and returned to Knox. Nine years later he married the niece of a theatrical acquaintance. She was Norah Cleveland and weighed some 170 pounds more than her 24-inch bridegroom, who stood on a table beside her during the ceremony.

The union seemed happy for almost fifteen years when it, too, ended in the divorce court. According to a story by Al Spiers, reporting for the *Circus Review*, Norah called Che-Mah "miserly, jealous, and ill-tempered." He testified that she had married him for his money. If so, she was disappointed. When Che-Mah died in 1926, at eighty-eight, Norah was given the remainder of his $30,000 estate, after a legal battle that dragged on for eight years and devoured most of her inheritance.

The name of Francis M. Uffner dropping into a conversation today would get you blank stares. But Uffner, too, was a

Major Joe Lessing, one of many "smallest men in circuit." (Circus World Museum, Baraboo, Wis.)

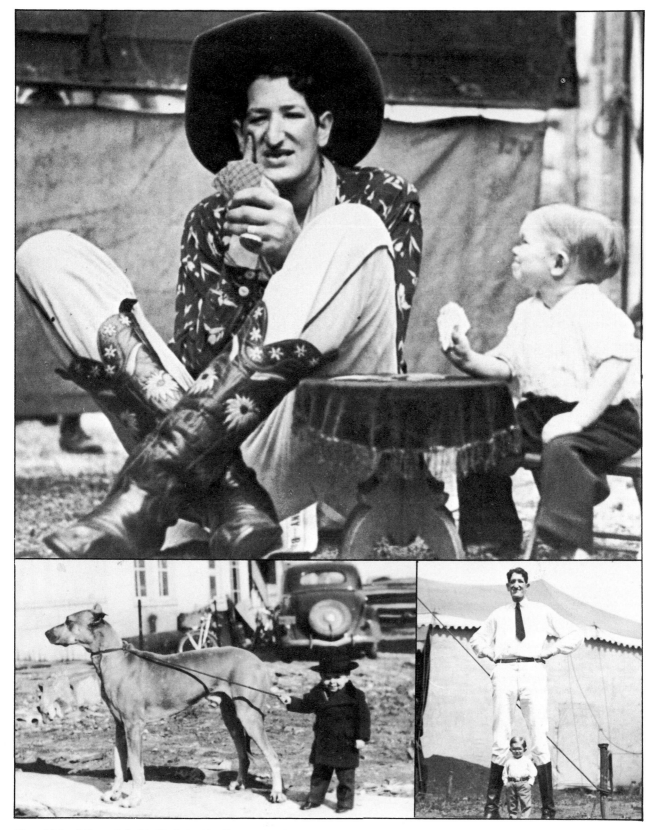

Top: Major Mite and Jackie Earle in friendly game, probably 1920's. Center: dog walking Major Mite. Bottom photo; the Major and the giant again. (Circus World Museum, Baraboo, Wis.)

famous showman during the waning years of the nineteenth century. He managed Dudley Foster, Admiral Dot, Jennie Quigley, Lucia Zarate, the Mexican Lilliputian, and her sister, sometimes billed as Cassie Foster. Uffner also handled the giant Colonel Bates, and Anna Swan, the noted giantess.

Foster, whose professional name was General Mite, was born in Nova Scotia. In 1866, when he was four years old and only 18 inches tall, his parents signed with George Starr for Dudley to appear at Bunnell's Curiosity Dime Museum in New York City.

Both the newly commissioned general and his midget sisters, who were part of the deal, were beautifully proportioned and very attractive. Midgets, indeed, are born with small but perfectly formed bodies. Dwarfs have a normal torso, but with large heads and short arms and legs. The terms, however, were often used interchangeably.

In 1882, if legends are to be believed, Foster had an affair with Adelina Patti, the opera star. According to the tale, the diva saw a photograph of the twenty-year-old General Mite outside of Bunnell's one day as she passed in her carriage, and promptly went in and "borrowed" the apparently willing Foster, now 22 inches high and about 10 pounds in weight.

Uffner took over Foster's contract during the 1890s, after he lost Lucia Zarate. Miss Zarate, billed as the Greatest Wonder of the Age, was born in 1864 in San Carlos, Mexico, and died when a Rocky Mountain blizzard halted the train on which she was traveling in 1890. At thirteen, Lucia was 20 inches high and weighed 5 pounds. Her arms reportedly were 8 inches long and her waist 14 inches around. At the peak of her career she earned an incredible twenty dollars an hour!

Sometime in the nineties General Mite seems to have slipped from view, although a new little person called Great Peter the Small, who bore startling resemblance to the general, subsequently appeared with Barnum and Bailey's Circus.

Dreamland Amusement Park, Coney Island, which burned down in 1907.

No dime museum was complete without one or more little people among its attractions. Colonel Woods Museum in Chicago, which was destroyed by the Great Fire of 1871, had at least three: Charles W. Nestel (Commodore Foote) and his sister, Elizabeth, the Fairy Queen, both out of Ft. Wayne, Indiana, and Joseph Hunter.

Another regular performer in museums from coast to coast was C. R. Decker, who during the Civil War years ran a newsstand in his native Nashville, Tennessee. Decker was born in 1855, and grew to 31 inches and 45 pounds from his birth weight of 8 pounds. He is said to have been a mechanical genius.

Beloit, Wisconsin, also sent one of its native sons into the entertainment world. His show-business name was General Carver, he was only 21 inches high, and he married

twenty-two years old, 17 inches high; Miss Rose, twenty-four years old, 24 inches; Miss Caroline, twenty-five, 25; Mr. Ernesto, twenty-three, 20; Mr. Paul, eighteen, 18; and Mr. Ferry was 21 inches tall.

For those who didn't like traveling, there eventually were such places as Leo Singer's Lilliputia, a complete Midget Village in Vienna, Austria; Mamid's Exposition Pier at Atlantic City, New Jersey; the World's Columbian Exposition in Chicago in 1893; a place in London known as Tiny Town; and Coney Island's Dreamland, which also had a small village called Lilliputia, among others. Unfortunately, even though Dreamland had its own fire department, that community burned down in 1907.

The world's fairs carried over into the twentieth century and were held in New York, San Diego, Chicago, and elsewhere. The Century of Progress Exposition on the Windy City's lakefront had a midget community with an elected mayor—a community run by the little people themselves during the many months of the fair.

But so far as their position in the entertainment world was concerned, the nineteenth century could rightly be called the Century of the Little People.

an older and very much larger woman, who also was a performer. In fact she was 456 pounds in weight, or more than 20 times as heavy as her husband. The two met in 1881 and were married the next year. Mme. Carver came from New Britain, Connecticut.

The Commodore was given a singular honor in 1862, when he was proclaimed by his fellows during a Washington convention as the smallest and most perfectly formed small person in the country. He was 37 inches tall, his sister 31, and Hunter 40.

There even were international troupes of little people, among them S. Horvath's Midgets, which toured the United States in 1886. The six members of the group were Hungarian and spoke Romanian, Russian, German, and Italian as well as their native language. Miss Anna was

Midget Village, Century of Progress Exposition, Chicago, 1933–1934.

Che-Mah. Despite exotic appearance, this Chinese little person yearned to be an Indiana farmer. The little lady posed with Che-Mah was named Pearley; she was not his wife. (Photos by Wendt and Eisenmann, New York City.)

On left page: Dudley Foster with his manager George Starr of Bunnell's Dime Museum, New York, c. 1870. Above: Lucia Zarate and manager Frank Uffner. Handbill showing Dudley Foster (also known as Gen. Mite) and Lucia Zarate, being held up by Frank Uffner, the Chicago showman.

Upper left: Dudley Foster, perhaps with parents. At right, Dudley at attention. At left, below, Lucia and Mother; to the right, Lucia and her sister. Right hand page, Lucia Zarate and a friend.

The Little Esquimaux Lady, Olaf Krarer of Greenland. (Photo by Bowman, Ottawa, Ill.)

Waino and Plutano, the so-called Wild Men of Borneo.

Waino and Plutano in three different poses; guardian, Hansford A. Warner and an etching from the booklet "Waino and Plutano, the Wild Men of Borneo."

Commodore Foote, Col. Small and Eliza Nestel. (Photo by Fredricks, New York City.)

Top left: Commodore Foote with sister Eliza Nestel, the Fair Queen, (Photo by Launey, Shelbyville, Ill. c. 1880.) Top right: sheet music cover of Commodore Foote and Col. Small. In the center Commodore Foote, Eliza Nestel, Col. Small. To the right, this carte de visite has written in back: "Col. Small dressed as woman."

Gen. Carver and large wife. The man on the left is presumably their manager. (Photo by Eisenmann.)

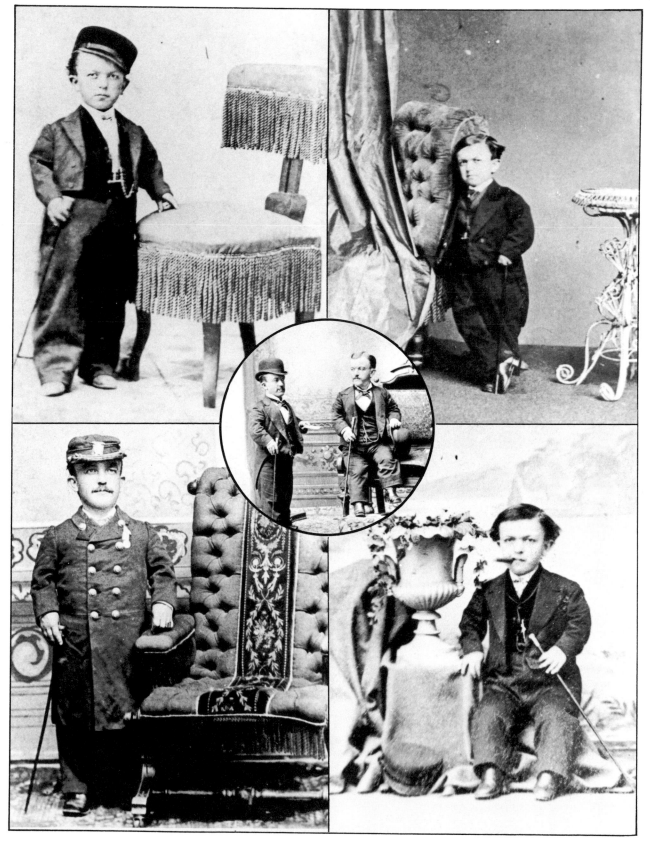

Charles Decker, of Nashville, Tenn., said to have been a mechanical genius. (Photos by Ranger, Syracuse, N.Y.)

Top left: S. Horvath's Midgets; Mr. Ernesto, Miss Caroline, Miss Rosie, Mr. Paul, Miss Anna, Mr. Ferry (Photo by Wendt, N.Y.C.) At bottom left: Rosie, Ernesto, Anna and Mr. Ferry, by Wendt. The large photo shows the S. Horvath Midgets with other sideshow attractions of the Barnum & Bailey Circus. Chang and Eng, the famed Siamese Twins, stand behind the little troupe. (Photo from the Charles King Coll.)

"Jack the Giant Killer" starred Ernest Rommell and Caroline Hass, with George Auger the huge figure at the back. Woman in center is unidentified. (Charles King Coll.)

Barnum's Little People

PHINEAS T. BARNUM WAS one of the greatest and most astute showmen who ever lived. Yet without Charles Sherwood Stratton it is probable that Barnum would have dwindled into the same obscurity that most of his rivals found.

Stratton, under the Barnum-bestowed name of General Tom Thumb, became world-famous and rich. Barnum himself, meanwhile, rode to even more lasting fame and fortune on the general's tiny coattails.

Barnum was a moderately successful entrepreneur when he decided to stop overnight in Bridgeport, Connecticut, in November 1842, where his half brother, Philo, was proprietor of the Franklin Hotel. The thirty-two-year-old Barnum had heard of an unusual child, a midget, living in town and asked Philo whether he could have him brought to the hotel.

This was done, and after a brief conversation during which the youngster overcame the shyness common to most five-year-olds, Barnum offered the parents, Sherwood and Cynthia Stratton, a con-

tract for their son's services. Sherwood was a carpenter, and the family needed money. The Strattons signed a four-week contract providing for the payment of three dollars weekly and all expenses for Charles and his mother.

Barnum had taken over the American Museum in New York less than a year before and was seeking new drawing cards. But the brief term of the initial contract indicates that even he did not realize what a superb attraction he had found.

There is controversy over the correct birth date of Charles S. Stratton, because of a typical Barnum trick. But even though *A Dictionary of American Biography,* published in Boston in 1876, gives the date as January 1832, it seems more probable he was born January 4, 1838.

The mix-up comes from the fact that when the boy and his mother reached New York on December 8, Barnum was already advertising his newest sensation: "Gen. Tom Thumb, a dwarf of 11 years, just arrived from England." He explained to the startled Mrs. Stratton that Americans preferred their entertainers from abroad and that if he gave the boy's age as five it would be assumed that he was simply small for his age and not a midget. He added that "Gen. Tom Thumb" had more appeal than "Charles Stratton."

In his earliest autobiography, published in 1855, Barnum tells of training Tom Thumb for his first public appearance, calling him "the most interesting and extraordinary natural curiosity of which the world has any knowledge."

As soon as General Tom Thumb opened at the American Museum the money began pouring in. Patrons flocked to see the 16-pound 25-inch miniature man in such numbers that when the four-week engagement was up, Barnum re-signed the mother and child for seven dollars weekly and a fifty-dollar bonus to be paid at the end of a year. The new contract stipulated that Tom could be shown anywhere in the United States. Barnum again paid all expenses, this time for both parents. Before the year ended the weekly wage was raised to twenty-five dollars, perhaps because Barnum had finished paying for the American Museum. A third contract called for fifty dollars weekly, with the option of a European tour.

No one ever said Barnum lacked flair. When he exercised the option for the trip abroad, the City Brass Band escorted the showman, the Strattons, and a French tutor, Professor Guillaudeu, to Sandy Hook, where they boarded the "new and splendid packet ship, *Yorkshire.*" It was the start of a three-year journey. Barnum dispatched one hundred letters to the *New York Atlas*, which had hired him as a correspondent, before the trip was over.

The *Yorkshire* docked at Liverpool nineteen days later, and Barnum, observing the large crowd waiting for a free glimpse of the little general, outwitted them by having Mrs. Stratton carry her son ashore in her arms as if he were an infant. The

showman's spirits were dampened quickly, however, when an English promoter that same day offered to engage Barnum and the boy for the equivalent of ten dollars a week. Another Englishman assured Barnum that he couldn't expect to charge more than a penny for a peep at Tom "for that is the usual price for seeing giants and dwarfs in England."

But the American booked his star for a brief run in a Liverpool theater, where the manager of the Princess Theater in London caught the act (a portion of which had Tom dressed and talking as if he were the Emperor Napoleon) and offered an engagement. Barnum cannily limited this to three nights, which proved to be wildly successful, then refused further offers. He rented a furnished house in the center of London and invited the nobility and several newspaper editors to call. Among the first week's visitors was Edward Everett, the American Minister, to whom Barnum suggested the idea of having Thumb introduced to Queen Victoria.

Shortly thereafter the Baroness Rothschild invited the Americans to her mansion, where they spent a couple of hours in the company of a score of lords and ladies. Barnum adds somewhat smugly: "On taking our leave, an elegant and well-filled purse was quietly slipped into my hand, and I felt that the golden shower was beginning to fall!"

After a second party invitation, this from Mr. Drummond, the banker, and a second well-filled purse, Barnum figured that the time had arrived. He hired Egyptian Hall in Piccadilly, and the announcement of a public appearance by General Tom Thumb brought a swarm of visitors. By now Barnum had dropped his dream of a summons to Buckingham Palace, since the Royal Family was mourning the death of Prince Albert's father.

But a few days later Ambassador Everett asked Barnum to breakfast with Charles Murray, Master of the Queen's Household, to whom Barnum mentioned that he planned to leave for the Continent shortly—adding that he would gladly postpone the trip if there were any chance of an audience with the Queen.

The invitation came quickly, accompanied by a suggestion from Her Royal Highness that there be no effort to instruct Tom in proper court protocol, since she wished him "to act naturally and without restraint." On the big night, patrons arriving at Egyptian Hall found this sign on the door:

"Closed this evening, General Tom Thumb being at Buckingham Palace by command of Her Majesty."

The affair went off without a hitch, even though Barnum disobeyed directions to address the Queen only through her lord-in-waiting, a gaffe which Queen Victoria herself graciously overlooked.

When Barnum and Tom were led into the palace picture gallery, where the Queen, Prince Albert, the Duchess of Kent, and a group of nobles awaited them, Thumb, "looking like a wax doll gifted with the power of locomotion," advanced on the group, bowed gracefully, and piped, in his high voice:

"Good evening, ladies and gentlemen!"

There was general laughter, and the Queen took her little guest by the hand and showed him the picture gallery, which Thumb pronounced "first rate." He then said he would like to see the Prince of Wales, which Queen Victoria promised would happen in the future. Then he sang, danced, and did his imitations.

The highlight of the evening came when the visitors left. All, including the diminutive general, were backing out of the royal presence, but whenever Tom found himself failing to keep up with the others, he would turn and run a few steps before resuming his formal withdrawal.

The running upset the Queen's poodle, which began barking at Tom, who retaliated by attacking the dog with his cane.

"A funny fight ensued," Barnum wrote later, "which renewed and increased the merriment of the royal party."

News stories about the Buckingham Palace visit increased public interest so much that Barnum hired a larger room in Egyptian Hall, and when a second and then a third invitation to appear at the Palace followed (during which Tom met the young Prince of Wales, measured himself against him, and said: "The Prince is taller than I am, but I *feel* as big as anybody"), Barnum remarks that "not to have seen Tom Thumb was voted to be decidedly unfashionable."

Ambrotype, believed hitherto unpublished, showing Tom Thumb, father and three brothers.

In consequence the admissions from March 20 through July 20 amounted to some five hundred dollars daily—a handsome profit as expenses for the same period were about fifty dollars daily. In addition to three public performances each day, Tom went to three or four private parties weekly, for which he was paid eight to ten guineas each.

There were other invitations also, including two from the Queen Dowager Adelaide at Marlborough House, where Tom was given a gold watch and chain—and a lecture on morals.

An indication of the intelligence of Tom Thumb, still not seven years old, may be had from his rejoinder to the Duke of Wellington, a frequent visitor, after the Iron Duke had seen Tom dressed in his Napoleon uniform, walking up and down in what seemed to be deep thought. The Duke asked what the boy was contemplating.

"I was thinking of the loss of the Battle of Waterloo," was the response.

In summing up the London visit, Barnum wrote that he did not believe a single member of the English nobility failed to see Tom in private, or at the exhibition hall. The American party had free entry to all theaters, public gardens, and other amusement centers, and met numerous writers and artists, including Albert Smith, who wrote a play called "Hop o' My Thumb," in which Thumb starred at the Lyceum and during a tour of the provinces.

There was a tragic accompaniment to Thumb's London triumph, however. A British painter, Benjamin Robert Haydon, sixty years old and in great financial straits, was exhibiting his painting "The Banishment of Aristides" in Egyptian Hall at the same time the general was attracting such great crowds. Haydon's work drew scant attention and little money and he eventually committed suicide. Although he had four times been in prison for debt, it seems to have been Tom's great popularity that was a contributing factor to Haydon's fatal depression. He left this note in his diary:

They rush by thousands to see Tom Thumb. They push, they fight, they scream, they faint, they cry help and murder! and oh! and ah! They see my bills, my boards, my caravans and don't read them. Their eyes are open, but their sense is shut. It is an insanity, a rabies, a madness, a furor, a dream. I would not have believed it of the English people.

Nathaniel Currier print of Tom Thumb. (Engraving by Napoleon Sarony.)

General Tom Thumb's appearances in Ireland, Scotland, and numerous places in France and Belgium were equally as successful as London had been. He had an audience with King Leopold and the Belgian Queen and four visits with King Louis-Philippe and the Royal Family in France. Honor followed honor in Paris, where Tom, in his little carriage, was in the royal procession on Longchamps Day.

Barnum mentions money once more: "I was compelled to take a cab to carry my bag of silver home at night."

Eventually, after watching Spanish bullfights with Isabella and dropping by Wa-

Early one-half plate daguerreotype of Tom Thumb and father, possibly taken by photographer John Plumbe, Jr., c. 1850. From the Len Walle Coll.

terloo to look at the battlefield, the party returned to London for further exhibitions and finally reached New York in February 1847, after an absence of more than three years.

General Tom Thumb promptly set new attendance records for the next month at the American Museum. He then went to Bridgeport on vacation, but agreed to be exhibited for two days in his hometown, contributing the money to the Bridgeport Charitable Association.

By this time Barnum and the general were equal partners in all of the latter's appearances, an arrangement made effective after January 1845. The elder Stratton, who looked after his son's earnings, put a large sum in the bank and spent $30,000 for land in Bridgeport on which he built a house for the family, which also included two daughters and a son, none economy-size.

In April Tom Thumb went on tour once again, visiting President Polk in the White House and extending the engagement throughout the South and to Cuba. In 1848 in Pittsburgh, Barnum and Thumb parted company. The promoter explained that he was weary of travel and would leave future bookings to his agents. He also opened a new museum in Philadelphia.

For the next thirteen years or so Charles Stratton (whose father died in 1855) did some exhibition work, but for the most part lived in semiretirement at his Bridgeport home, where he engaged in business deals and spent time at his billiard table or on his yacht. In 1862, however, he paid a visit to the American Museum, where Barnum had just placed under contract a very attractive and very small young lady named Mercy Lavinia Warren Bump.

Love seems to have struck Tom at first sight of the "little lady of very fair proportions, decidedly of the plump style of beauty, with a well-rounded arm and full bust." There were complications, however. Barnum had signed up another minuscule man, George Washington Nutt, now eighteen years old and 29 inches high, who also was in love with Lavinia. Rivalry between the two men became so intense that there were reports of a fistfight in which Commodore Nutt, as Barnum had renamed him, knocked his more corpulent rival down.

Barnum had no objections to a romantic merger between Tom and Lavinia, and the smitten general, after showing Lavinia around his hometown, and convincing her suspicious mother that the match was a suitable one, persuaded the little beauty to become engaged.

The pair then began appearing together at the museum, and drew such multitudes that Barnum tried to persuade them to postpone the wedding for a few weeks. They refused.

The ceremony took place on February 10, 1863, in Grace Church, New York City. Minnie Warren Bump, Lavinia's sister, also a little person, was bridesmaid, and invitations to the affair were at a premium, with some of the would-be guests offering

Pre-Civil War photo of New York shoeshine boys. Note poster in background advertising Gen. Tom Thumb.

as much as fifty dollars for one. New York society was on hand, and the guests included Major General Ambrose L. Burnside and, of course, P. T. Barnum.

General Thumb wore "a full dress suit of the finest broadcloth, vest of corded silk, with blue silk under vest, and shining boots." Lavinia's bridal gown was "of snowy satin, its skirt, fashioned with a flowing train, decorated with a superb point lace flounce which cost its half hundred a yard." She also wore a diamond star just above her forehead.

Commodore Nutt, a good sport in defeat, was best man.

Among those who sent wedding gifts were President and Mrs. Lincoln, Mr. and Mrs. August Belmont, and scores of other personages. The wedding presents included a miniature silver tea set from Mrs. James Gordon Bennett, wife of the publisher; a richly carved foot-high rosewood chair, upholstered in blue velvet; a diamond ring, this from Commodore Nutt; a gold-handled fan made of feathers; and a miniature silver horse and chariot from Tiffany's.

Not to be outdone, Barnum gave the newlyweds a casket made of tortoiseshell from which, when a spring was pressed, arose a tiny bird with genuine feathers, which moved its wings and sang. The item came from London and cost five hundred dollars.

Not everyone saw this glittering event with pleasure. The diary of Maria Lydig Daly, a rather acidulous Unionist who was the wife of a New York judge and observed her times with more candor and prejudice than kindness, reveals that she felt the wedding cheapened the church it was held in:

> The city has been greatly amused and excited at the marriage of Tom Thumb and Lavinia Warren, the two dwarfs, and I think our Episcopal Church has disgraced herself by marrying them in such pomp in Grace Church. There could not have been more done had they been some distinguished personages. Poor Brown, the sexton, was so disgusted that he would not be present, and the police took his place. He told us when opening the carriage door for us at Judge Bell's reception that Bishop

British stereograph shows Tom Thumb with member of the palace guard. Probably taken on Thumb's first trip to Europe.

Potter had asked Dr. Taylor for the church. Another lady told me that Dr. Taylor received $500 for the use of the church, which now I think is on a par with Barnum's Museum.

The honeymoon journey included stops in Philadelphia, Baltimore, and Washington, where the couple stayed at Willard's Hotel and visited the White House. This was one of the first receptions Mrs. Lincoln held after her long period of mourning for Willie Lincoln, who had died in 1862. The novelty of the honored pair must have made the occasion easier for Mary Lincoln to face the public after many months. Lavinia wore diamonds and a white satin gown, made by Madame Demorest, New York's leading designer. The dress was looped with carnation buds and green leaves. Tom Thumb, to be sure, was resplendent, too, in patent-leather shoes, white kid gloves, and a "sparkling breastpin" to complete his outfit. Robert Lincoln refused to come downstairs to meet the famous little people, but the President and his wife welcomed them warmly. A number of Lincoln biographers have recorded that the President was not only very courteous but also gentle. A Grace Greenwood who was present later wrote of their meeting with Lincoln: "With profound respect they looked up, up, to the President's face. It was pleasant to see their tall host bend, and bend, to take their little hands in his great palm, holding Madame's with special chariness, as though it were a robin's egg, and he were afraid of breaking it."

Tom Thumb's brother, as a soldier in the 40th Massachusetts Regiment, was one of the defenders of the Capital and possibly was present at the reception. Later the Thumbs were almost mobbed at a dance held at Willard's hotel.

Although Tom Thumb was Barnum's chief attraction, many other miniature entertainers appeared for him. Nutt, whom Stratton edged in the Lavinia sweepstakes, was one of the most important.

He was born in 1844 on a New Hampshire farm. By the time Barnum discovered him in 1862 inflation had hit the midget market and the promoter had to pay $200 a week, plus expenses, and promise other monies from the sale of autographed books and photos. Because the contract guaranteed $30,000 over three years, the eighteen-year-old 24-pounder became known as "the $30,000 Nutt."

Curiously, Nutt bore a close resemblance to General Tom Thumb as he had looked before his face became pumpkin-round, so that many of the museum patrons believed that Nutt *was* Thumb, when they saw him alone. Barnum capitalized on this suspicion by recalling the General from his western tour and displaying both men at once. Even this failed to convince many, who were certain that Nutt was Thumb and that Thumb was an impostor.

Nutt also was invited to the White House, where he and Barnum met and chatted with President Lincoln and his Cabinet. Lincoln, in bidding his guests farewell, said:

"Commodore, permit me to give you a parting piece of advice. When you are in command of your fleet, if you find yourself in danger of being taken prisoner, I advise you to wade ashore."

Nutt was unabashed as he gazed up at the gangling Lincoln.

"I guess, Mr. President," he said, "that you could do better than I could."

Barnum also signed Minnie Bump, Lavinia's younger sister, who accompanied the Thumbs on their round-the-world trip. Minnie, an actress, was slightly smaller than Lavinia. In 1874 she married Major Edward Newell, an English exhibition skater, who was below average height. When Minnie became pregnant in her first year of marriage, her doctors told her that to save her life they would have to destroy the baby. She pleaded that she did not want to live if the child could not. She died about a year after the wedding in childbirth, with her baby.

Thumb as Napoleon, one of his many roles.

Tom in Scottish uniform. (London Stereoscopic Co.)

Another of Barnum's naval attractions was Admiral Dot, also known as the Eldorado Elf (born Leopold Kahn in San Francisco), who traveled with the great impresario's new circus, launched in 1871.

The acquisition of another possible replacement for Tom Thumb, which occurred when Leopold's parents brought their 24-inch son to meet Barnum in California, was announced to W. C. Coup, Barnum's partner in "the Greatest Show on Earth," in a letter sent October 8, 1870:

> My dear Coup: Yours received. I will join you in a show for next Spring and will probably have Admiral Dot (Thumb's successor) well trained this winter and have him and Harrington in the show. . . . You can have a Cardiff Giant that won't crack, also a moving figure, Sleeping Beauty or Dying Zouave—a big gymnastic figure like that in Wood's Museum, and lots of other good things, only you need time to look them up and prepare wagons, etc., etc.

Admiral Dot was decked out quickly in a British naval uniform and exhibited in San Francisco. He later wed a tiny lady, Lottie Swartwood, who was an inch taller than Dot, and finally became a hotel-keeper in White Plains, New York, after twenty years on the road. During his career the Admiral was billed as the world's smallest man, and also as the smallest quick-change artist in the world. He was with the Lilliputian Opera Company with Jennie Quigley, the Scottish Princess, and with Mrs. Tom Thumb. Another touring midget, Major Atom, was a nephew of Admiral Dot.

Barnum was among several promoters who were happy to exhibit Major Tot Porter during his career. Born in Fitchburg, Massachusetts, Tot is *said* to have been small enough to sleep stretched out on his mother's hand when he was seven months old, and to have begun to talk at nine

Studio-posed shot by Brady of bridal couple with Commodore Nutt and Minnie, Lavinia's sister.

Posed wedding group, (From Brady negative.)

months. While his age is unknown in January 1865, it *is* known that he was 28 inches tall and weighted only 10 pounds.

Tot, also known as Totman, the Prince Lilliputian, and the Little Wonder (and no wonder), appeared at the Boylston Museum in Boston in 1875, under the managership of John Hopkins, and contracted measles that same year. Again the date is vague, but sometime later (and obviously while Tot was still a youngster) Barnum paid Hopkins and the parents handsomely for the privilege of showing Major Tot Porter at the corner of Broadway and Thirty-fifth Street in New York.

Unfortunately, Barnum displayed Tot in a refrigerated building which also held the live fish display, and Tot's folks feared he might pick up some ailment from the cold. They paid Barnum to break the contract. A brochure about Tot Porter has found a home at the Chicago Historical Society, and in it are listed ten reasons for viewing the Little Wonder. The sixth is most convincing: "Because P. T. Barnum and all other great showmen are now, and for years have been, offering large sums for his services, which proves he is a great curiosity."

Others who worked for Barnum and who seem worthy of at least a passing reference include Susie Reed and General Grant, Jr., who usually were shown alongside a pair of giants, Noah Orr and Routh Goshen. Miss Reed (or Read), at twenty-two, was 33 inches high and weighed 25 pounds. General Grant, Jr., at fourteen, was 21 inches high and 18 pounds in weight.

When Barnum's American Museum burned on July 13, 1865, Anna Swan, the Nova Scotia Giantess, was overcome by smoke. Her best friend, the Living Skeleton, remained with the 8-foot 1-inch Anna, while Miss Reed and the General ran for help. Miss Reed later appeared with Mrs. Tom Thumb in the Lilliputian Opera Company.

Carrie Akers, the wee fat lady, was another of Barnum's little attractions, as were Partial H. Kinney and Nellie Keller, who appeared at the American Museum in 1863. Miss Keller was 28 inches tall and weighed 12 pounds at the age of eleven.

Chiquita (the Cuban Atom or the Living Doll) also spent some time on Barnum's payroll. She was born in Erie, Pennsylvania, but claimed Cuba as her

native country. It is said that at birth her chest was 3 inches wide, her head 2¾ inches across, her legs less than 4 inches in length, and her hands barely more than an inch wide. She grew up to be 29 inches high, however, and was noted as a singer as well as entertainer. In 1901 she wed Tony Woeckler, a bandleader of normal size.

Also star attractions in the late Nineteenth century were twin sisters, who never appeared under Barnum's auspices, but did know or work with many of the little people who did. They were Lucy and Sarah Adams, born on Martha's Vineyard in the late 1860s. Lucy was 49 inches tall at maturity and Sarah 46 inches, and they were friends of General Tom Thumb and his wife late in Thumb's career. The sisters were charming and held to their convictions: they refused a trip to Europe because it would have meant working on Sunday. They were very popular on the Chautauqua circuit, where they sometimes appeared with William Jennings Bryan, and retired to Martha's Vineyard in 1917.

Barnum lost his New American Museum, again by fire, on March 3, 1868, and announced his retirement. But the showman was restless without his work. In 1870 he signed Kahn in San Francisco, and in 1871 Barnum and Coup began their highly successful circus. His final triumph came in 1889 when he took a huge circus for a European tour. He returned to the United States in 1890, soon fell ill, and died April 7, 1891.

He is buried in Mountain Grove Cemetery in Bridgeport, where his friend and greatest attraction, General Tom Thumb, also rests.

Engraving from Harper's Weekly showing Gen. and Mrs. Thumb and Minnie Warren Bump leaving for Europe on Oct. 24, 1864. Judging by traveling garb, this was taken the same day.

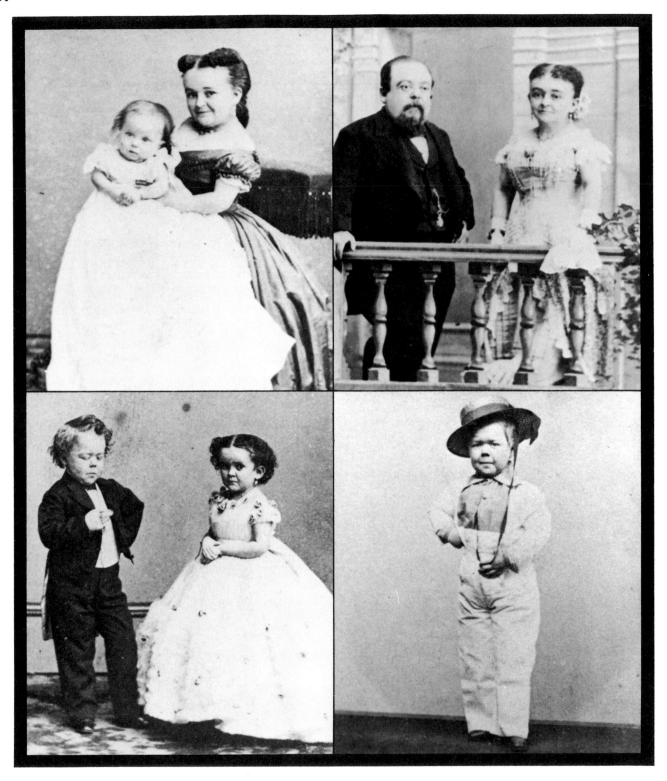

Top left: a Barnum hoax; Lavinia never had a baby. (Brady Photo.) Top right; the aging Tom and Lavinia shown on studio "balcony." (Bogardus, N.Y.C.) At bottom left, Commodore and Minnie Bump. To the right, the Commodore dressed as sailor. On right hand page, P. T. Barnum with his "$30,000 Nutt." (Photo by Brady.)

The Commodore strikes a military pose for Matthew Brady's camera.

Leopold Kahn (Admiral Dot) with his parents, Mr. and Mrs. Gabriel Kahn of San Francisco.

At left: Admiral Dot and unknown friend. (Bradley and Rulofson Photo, San Francisco.) At right: this Charles Meier cabinet card shows nine of the costumes in Admiral Dot's quick-change sequence. (Meier, St. Louis.)

Major Tot with manager in photo above and posed alone in lower study. (Photos by W. R. Babcock, Toledo, O., and Joseph G. Morris, Pittsburgh Pa.)

General Grant, Jr., perched uneasily on the guard of sword held by Col. Routh Goshen, Barnum's Arabian Giant. (Photo by Bailey and Silvers, N.Y.)

Rare carte de visite shows 11 of Barnum's American Museum attractions, including Suzie Reed and General Grant Jr. Large photo shows Suzie Reed with giant, Noah Orr, who bore a close resemblance to Goshen.

Partial H. Kinney, the Lilliputian King. (Brady Photo.)

Carrie Akers, Barnum's Fat lady/little person. Face at window appears to be Hansford A. Warner, who was guardian for the Wild Men of Borneo.

Chiquita, "the living doll," poses against a wintry backdrop for Elmer Chickering, the Boston photographer.

Sarah and Lucy Adams of Martha's Vineyard. (Photo by Oliver, N.Y.C.)

Barnum's dwarf from India and Nellie Keller (Miss Keller from Charles King Coll.)

Count and Countess Magri. She was formerly Mrs. Tom Thumb. (Photo by Oliver, N.Y.C.)

Lavinia and the Count

HEN GENERAL TOM Thumb died in 1883 at his home in Connecticut, his widow was not so well-off financially as she would have been a few years earlier. Some of the general's investments had been ill advised, and Lavinia found herself with not much more than $16,000 and the Bridgeport house, now in need of repairs.

It seems certain that she and Stratton had loved each other very much. Paradoxically, this may have been one reason why she remarried two years after his death. She probably found life too lonely without him. A second reason may have been that her new husband, a little showman whose name was Count Primo Magri, was an old friend who also bore a startling resemblance to Tom Thumb. Lavinia was forty-two and the Count thirty-four.

Count Primo Magri, whose title was a papal one, was born Guiseppe Magri in Bologna, Italy. He was a fine boxer and excellent piano and piccolo player, whose adult height was 45 inches. Primo and his brother, Ernesto, eight years younger, were the sons of Santo Magri, also diminutive,

who had appeared on the Italian carnival circuit. Despite having fathered thirteen children with his normal-size wife, Santo reputedly had an eye for the ladies.

The Count and Ernesto, also known as Baron Magri, had done an act for many years in the United States as Count Rosebud and Baron Littlefinger, and a story in *Clipper* magazine for May 2, 1885, indicates that Ernesto was following his father's life-style in more ways than one. He was arrested on a paternity charge, brought by a Miss Ida Newman, not short, who swore that the Baron had promised to marry her, then declared that he was unable to do so because of having a wife and family in Italy. Although the Baron insisted that Miss Newman made the advances, he was ordered to pay her two hundred dollars.

With some worries about money, then, it was natural for the widow of the renowned Tom Thumb to return to show business. She and the two Magris formed the Lilliputian Opera Company and took to the road.

Advertising handbill and Mrs. Tom Thumb (with dog.) (Photo by L. B. Wilson, 1893.)

The Baron could sing and dance, and played several musical instruments well. Others who became members of the troupe included Admiral Dot, Major Atom, Chiquita, the Adams Sisters, and the exquisite Jennie Quigley, the Scottish Princess.

Jennie, who was the same age as Lavinia, was born in Glasgow, Scotland. When she was eighteen years old, she stood 28 inches high and weighed only 32 pounds. She came to the United States via sailing ship in 1865, after having appeared before Queen Victoria and other European rulers, and had played Chicago just after the Great Fire of 1871. She was one of the great little ladies of show business, and was billed as the smallest lady vocalist in the world. Superlatives had already made a permanent place for themselves in the vocabulary of the spotlight and tinsel crowd, but in the case of Miss Quigley even the

most extravagant of claims seem to have been justified.

The roster of the Lilliputian Opera Company was a long one, including, over the years, Colonel R. A. Steere, who eventually was a part owner; his wife, Rebecca Ann; General and Ida Totman; Sarah E. Belton, a familiar figure in dime museums during the nineties; Major Newell, widower of Minnie Bump; Colonel Speck, born Frank Springer; Major Davis, a fair country tenor; Count DeKay; Prince Louis, later to take his juggling skills to the Gulliver Lilliputians; Rebecca Meyers of Marshall County, Indiana, a singer; and Emma Bernhardt, a soprano. One of the productions staged was the opera *Pocahontas*, a perennial favorite for many seasons.

As the opera troupe became less of an attraction, Lavinia and the two brothers

Top left: Count Rosebud and Baron Littlefinger, who was later known as Count Magri and Baron Magri. (Photo by L. B. Wilson, 1893.) At right: the Baron disguised as a woman. Bottom left: Count Magri, as Swiss Miss, scolding the Baron in a comic skit. To the right, Baron Littlefinger, his wife, and daughter, Ila; son Iro, and seated son, Leo. Count Rosebud (Count Magri) is on far left. (Photo by Oliver, N.Y.C.)

developed their own act. During the off season the Count and Countess headed for Bridgeport, where they opened the Tom Thumb house to public view, for a fee. They also added to their income with an ice-cream parlor named Primo's Pastime. But when the warm days came, they went back to the world they knew best.

In 1893 both Lavinia and Jennie Quigley were among the little people appearing at the World's Columbian Exposition in Chicago, and the latter then made Chicago her permanent residence. Lavinia also played the Great Chicago Museum during this period. It was a block north of the Clark Street bridge, and since this was to be her final appearance, Lavinia handed out cards to each visitor. They read:

> Having exhibited at all the finest theatres at home and abroad and being about to leave for the east, I desire to say goodbye from the Great Chicago Museum, which I consider one of the largest and most complete places of amusement in the world. I would therefore respectfully announce that this is my last and farewell week here, and I take this method of wishing my many friends a Merry Christmas and a Happy New Year. Very respectfully, Mrs. General Tom Thumb.

An idea of the atmosphere greeting those who worked in the dime museums, at least in Chicago at the end of the nineteenth century, may be had from a book called *Chicago by Day and Night: The Pleasure Seeker's Guide to the Paris of America* (Chicago, 1892), which does not list an author's name. This is the pertinent excerpt:

> THE DIME MUSEUMS. Chicago is probably more bountifully supplied than any other city in the Dime Museum line. It is not necessary to particularize as to the various houses of this character; they are scattered in all quarters of the city, and in them is to be found infinite material for entertainment and instruction at the modest admission fee of 10 cents. The freaks of all climes are to be found on exhibition and most of the museums throw in a stage per-

formance of some kind more or less meritorious.

> A favorite plan of a party, large or small, desirous of a little quiet fun, is to execute a "Dime Museum Raid," as it is called. They assemble at the hotel or other meeting place, and start out on a tour of the various museums, visiting each in turn, with, of course, the usual intermission for drinks. The amount of fun to be obtained from such an excursion can easily be imagined. Aside from the entertainment to be derived from viewing the freaks on exhibition, it is a very easy matter to discover food for mirth in the freaks among the audience.

> There is a happy-go-lucky atmosphere in a Dime Museum which is not found elsewhere, and the Dime Museum "raiders" are in the habit of getting much more than their money's worth; but so long as their fun does not end in a fight, there need be no cause for complaint.

The Magris grow older; Above left; Count points at Lavinia (note dog again) as unknown in background points at the Count, and the Baron slouches against table. (Photo by Eisenmann.)

A thing that should be looked into is the attendance at certain of these cheap shows of young girls whose tender youth leads one to marvel why their parents do not manage to keep them home, or, failing that, to box their ears and send them to bed for their contumacy. It is not the province of the writer, however, to purify the morals of this great and growing town, so let those "kick" who will.

Coney Island and a sideshow in the Dreamland Amusement Park seem to have been the next stops on what must have seemed like a downhill slide to Lavinia and her husband. They lived on the grounds, in their own small place, but the memories must have been bitter ones. Luckily, Wee Willie Archie showed up a few years later—perhaps around 1911 or so. He was still in his teens, but already the world's smallest (4 feet 6 inches) and youngest booking agent.

Archie took them on as clients, and found them roles with his Pee Wee Players in several motion pictures. He also got them vaudeville bookings. Archie, born in New York City in 1894, went onto the stage early, and by 1912 was appearing opposite Lillian Russell in *Wildfire*. He also is said to have introduced Miss Russell to Alexander Moore, her future husband. Archie played with Weber and Fields, and was in the Music Box Revue and the Ziegfeld Follies.

At his busiest, Wee Willie represented about 125 little people performers, and in 1932 he found jobs for his Pee Wee Players in a radio drama starring Meyer Berenson, a little person from the Yiddish theater in New York City. Berenson, who was 3 feet 11 inches tall at the time, eventually grew up to be 4 feet 11 and, as Wee Willie put it: "He grew out of his job." Berenson had also starred in an early Biograph production with an unknown named Mary Pickford.

Baron Magri died in 1914, by which time Lavinia and the Count had disposed of the Bridgeport property and moved to Marion, Ohio, hometown of President Warren G. Harding, where they lived in retirement in a house built to their subnormal needs, a retirement disturbed only by sightseers—paying ones, of course—who dropped by from time to time. When Lavinia was old, Irving Wallace tells us in his fine biography *The Fabulous Showman*, she "grew fat and garrulous, and much devoted to Christian Science and the D.A.R."

Lavinia died in 1919, still wearing a locket with Tom Thumb's photograph in it. Count Magri died about two years later. Lavinia, at her request, was buried in Bridgeport, very close to the monument to General Tom Thumb. The words on her grave are short and simple. They read:

"His Wife"

Count Magri and his Countess in early Ford

The Lilliputian Opera Co. Left to right, Admiral Dot, Jennie Quigley, Major Davis, Sarah Belton, Col. Speck and (seated) Rebecca Steers. (photo by C. W. Jeffrey, Boston, Mass.) Inset, Advertisement for the Lilliputian Opera.

THE ONLY Liliputian Opera

Left page, Montage of Jennie Quigley, the Scottish Queen. Right page photo at top left shows Jennie with Admiral Dot. Jeffrey of Boston.) To the right, Jennie dressed as Oriental. Bottom left and right, Jennie as Jennie.

Col. Bob Steere, above left. To the right, Rebecca Ann Steere. (Bogardus photos, N.Y.C.); Major Davis (W. H. Owen, Scranton, Pa.). Below, Sarah E. Belton (Webster, Louisville, Ky.) Princess Ida and husband, Gen. Totman (Boston Photogravure Co.); the demure Rebecca Myer (W. O. Connor, Toronto, Can., c. 1870.)

Major Don Cameron

Artists, Photographers, and the Little People

THE EARLIEST PORTRAY-als of little people were the statues, stone carvings, and frescoes made by artists in Egypt and Rome many centuries ago. A close inspection of the walls of Pompeii, a town buried in molten lava in A.D. 79, reveals depictions of small people doing some of the things that the residents of Pompeii seem to have enjoyed doing, to put it delicately.

The sketch-artists and painters were next, and some extremely fine oil paintings survive from Velázquez, Goya, Paolo Veronese, Mantegna, Domenichino, Vandycke, Brueghel, and the Russian Vasili Vereshchagin, who specialized in battle and execution scenes and died in 1904 when Admiral Makarov's flagship, *Petropavlovsk*, was sunk off Port Arthur, during the Russo-Japanese conflict.

Literary illustrations, for such works as *Gulliver's Travels*, John Ruskin's *The King of the Golden River*, or stories for children about the Yellow Dwarf, popular during the late nineteenth century, also were common, as were newspaper and magazine illustrations of little people in the era before photography was invented, and even later.

Among the unusual artwork dealing with the subminiature person is that found on sheet music. "The Fairy Bride Polka," for example, composed in 1864 by G. R. Cromwell, is dedicated to Lavinia Warren (Mrs. Tom Thumb). The lithograph on the cover page, showing Tom and his bride, with Commodore Nutt and Minnie Bump, and the minister standing behind them, was by Major and Knapp of New York, former partners of Napoleon Sarony. The artist, obviously, has used the famous Brady photograph of the ceremony as a model.

Another song sheet is "The Commodore Foote and Fairy Queen March," written in 1880 by E. M. Mack and published by H. Keyser, Philadelphia. The illustration shows Foote, in civvies, standing beside his sister, Eliza Nestel. Both seem middle-aged. W. F. Shaw did the artwork.

Major Mite, not even twice as tall as Graflex camera. (Circus World Museum, Baraboo, Wis.)

Singer's Midgets on the road.

Other similar pieces of sheet music include "The Dance of the Midgets" (1898), published by Will Wood, New York, which has two little persons in elfin costume watching seven others, similarly attired, dancing. This was intended for the use of music students. And finally there was "The City Museum Polka," by Adolph Scherzer, inspired by Barnum's American Museum. This, too, was published in Philadelphia, about 1864 or '65.

There had been other faintly successful experiments in photography, but not until 1839 did the photographic era really begin. Then Louis Jacques Mandé Daguerre, a painter, announced the daguerreotype, also known as "the mirror with a memory," since the picture was fixed on highly polished silver. Daguerre's announcement (made by a friend on January 7) was followed on January 25 by the revelation that an Englishman, William Henry Fox Talbot, had found a method of making a photographic image on paper instead of metal. Talbot called the result a calotype, but a more popular name was the talbotype. Eventually both methods were replaced, but they had launched a new art form.

In consequence, daguerreotypes of little people are now very rare, and highly collectible, especially one showing Tom Thumb. It became popular for dime muse-

ums, including Peale's in New York City, to hire daguerreotypists to give demonstrations of this curious new process, although no daguerreotype known to have been processed in a dime museum has come to public notice.

Dime Museum entertainer, Prince Napoleon.
(Wendt Photo, N.Y.C.)

In 1843 Barnum himself took his tiny general to the John Plumbe Jr. National Daguerreian Gallery at 251 Broadway, in New York City, where Thumb sat for several different portraits. One of these, according to Cliff Krainek of Arlington Heights, Illinois, an authority on Plumbe

Painting by Velazquez (1599–1660) in Museo del Prado, Madrid, Spain.

and old photographs, was used by Nathaniel Currier in the making of an 1846 lithograph.

The daguerreotype shows Charles Stratton standing on a chair beside a male figure, probably his father. But Currier has removed the man, in his lithograph, which simply has Tom Thumb standing alone on a chair. The artist used by Currier for adapting the original was Napoleon Sarony, who worked for Currier from 1840 to 1846 before opening his own lithographic studio. The lithograph, as it finally was printed, shows Thumb standing in front of a curtain. Around the sides are thirteen pictures of Tom in as many different stage costumes. It is headed: "Barnum's Gallery of Wonders No. 1" and was the start of a series.

Sarony, whose photographs also are highly prized by image collectors today, eventually became a familiar figure in

New York. He was only a little over dwarf size himself, at 5 feet 1, and often wore a jacket of calfskin, riding breeches, and shiny cavalry boots, the whole set off by a Turkish fez. Visitors to his gallery—almost a museum in itself—had to learn to ignore a large stuffed crocodile leering down from the ceiling. Sarony turned to photography in 1864.

By the Civil War period the *carte de visite,* a photograph printed on a card, about 2½ by 4 inches, had become very popular. Since these were inexpensive to produce (a photographer in Paris had learned how to shoot several poses on the same plate), they were admirably adapted for such purposes as making photographs of dime museum celebrities, which explains why autographed CDVs of Tom Thumb and other noted little people are fairly common.

Colonel Speck, a little person, showman and photographer of his period.

Ambro-type, circa 1854, of Mrs. Shade, performer.

By 1866, however, the Cabinet Photo had arrived, in a much larger format (about 4½ by 6 inches), and demand for the *cartes de visite* slackened quickly. As a result business was brisk at such places as the Jeremiah Gurney, Bogardus, and Matthew Brady galleries in New York. So admired was the work of Brady, who became famous for his Civil War photographs, that his *cartes de visite* were pirated by lesser-known photographers across the country and used to make prints of Brady's well-known subjects under the local photographer's imprint. One of the major distributors of Brady's work was E. and H. T. Anthony, who also made cameras and photo supplies.

There seems to have been a natural affinity between the dime museums and big-city photographic studios. Charles Eisenmann, a twenty-six-year-old immigrant from Germany, bought out a studio in the heart of the Bowery from Peter Kohlbeck in 1876, at 229 Bowery. This was close to the New Wonderland Museum, 138 Bowery; Vananburgh's Palace of Wonders Museum, 103 Bowery; George Dixon's Vaudeville Theater; and the People's Theater. Eisenmann's place was across the street from David Yesky, The American Tailor, and Houlihan the Shoemaker, who must have added a bit of tone to the neighborhood.

Eisenmann quickly became the semiofficial photographer for the theaters and dime museums. Sometime in the 1880s he took on a partner, Frank Wendt. When the studio began paying off, a branch was opened in a better part of town, where Eisenmann photographed P. T. Barnum. By

1885 Eisenmann seems to have been an automatic choice for any of the little people wishing to be photographed, and visitors to the studio already had included Major Mite, the Adams Sisters, Dudley Foster, and Chiquita.

Business must have fallen off in the next few years, which may explain the change of studio name to the Royal Photographic Company shortly after the turn of the century. The keenest competition in the Bowery probably was the Joseph Woods Gallery, although there were other studios within easy range: Oliver's at 343 Sixth Avenue and the Pachmann Brothers Gallery, near Fifth Avenue and Twenty-third Street.

The S. Horvath Midgets went to Pachmann's in 1906, when the Barnum and Bailey Circus was in town. By 1912 the New York City business directory, for the first time in many years, failed to list an Eisenmann enterprise. He, Wendt, and the Royal Photographic Company, all were gone.

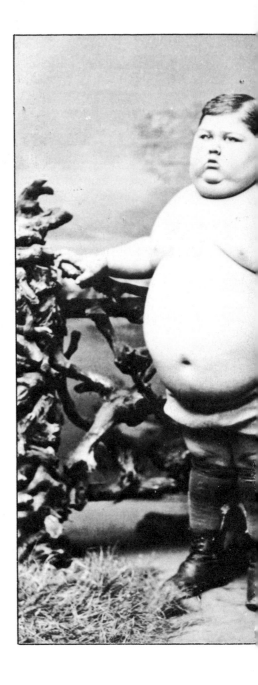

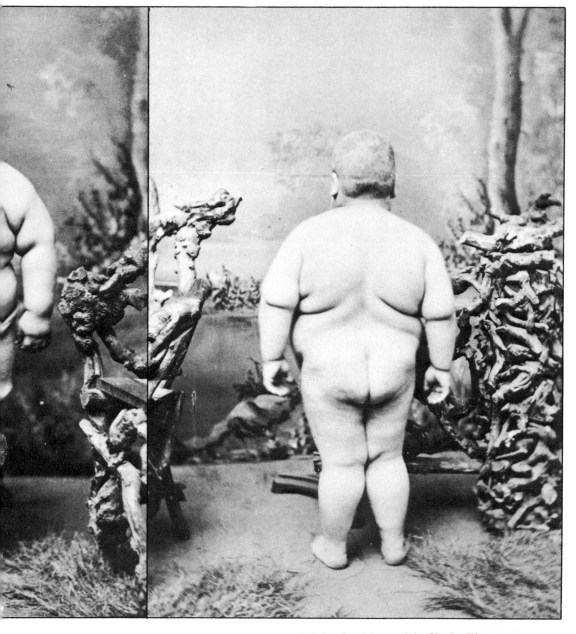

*At left, advertising card for Charles Eisenmann, one
of the most popular photographers of little people. To
the right; photographer Frank Wendt (Boonton, N.J.)
makes unpleasant shots of fat little unknown.*

Eisenmann next surfaced in Plainfield, New Jersey, as a dealer in photographic supplies. Wendt moved to Boonton, New Jersey, where he opened a photo studio. Not much is known about either man thereafter. It is possible that Wendt worked for Pachmann's, who specialized in school photography, but this is a guess. It is known, however, that Wendt brought some of the old glass negatives from the Bowery and made new prints. Never the craftsman that Eisenmann was, however, Wendt unwittingly devised a means for collectors to tell his stuff at a glance. Most of the Wendt prints are poorly fixed, and as a result badly faded and a sharp contrast to Eisenmann's crisp product.

Many image collectors today would like to know more about the career and personal life of Charles Eisenmann, and some have tried to gather data, but the pickings have been slim. It is probably Eisenmann's photograph on the back of some of his work, showing a young-looking man dressed in what may be the clothes of an artist or a photographer. The figure is running, his feet on a globe of the world. The inscription under the illustration reads: "Charles Eisenmann, the Popular Photographer."

It is known that Eisenmann was married and the father of a daughter. But there must be more information somewhere.

Many of the illustrations, photographic or sketched, were done by artists or photographers who worked for various circuses. Two lithographers, Charles Parks and George Hedges, are listed as employees of Barnum and Bailey in 1906, a year in which the sideshow attractions included the little people of Gulliver's Midgets and S. Horvath's Lilliputians. Among these were Colonel Page, the Shortest Man on Earth; Ernest Rommell, the world's smallest comedian; and Carolina Hass, the Smallest Sketch Artist in the World, who appeared in a sketch called "Jack the Giant-Killer," with Rommell and a circus giant, George Auger.

Also with the 1906 Barnum and Bailey was Charles Andress, a photographer, to whom a poem, "The Ol' Pho'graph Man," was written by Willard Coxey and printed (all six stanzas) in the route book.

Carolina Hass, it should be added, was also known as Helen Louise Haskell and was the first wife of Joe Short, who later was seen at the 1934 Chicago World's Fair with Elsie Schultz, his second wife.

Imitation Tom Thumb pose by enterprising photographer C. M. Pierce, Leominster, Mass.

Herbert Barnett, also known as Dainty Demdrops and Admiral Thumb. (About 1900.)

Spies, Scholars, Military and Religious Leaders, and Politicians

JEFFREY HUDSON WAS born in 1619 and died in 1682. During that span of time he entered the service of Queen Henrietta Maria, was twice captured by pirates, shot and killed a man in a duel, grew 21 inches after the age of thirty, and was imprisoned briefly on suspicion of being involved in the Popish Plot of Titus Oates.

He also was made a Captain of Horse by Charles I of England, and may even have been knighted by the King, though probably in jest.

Hudson was born in Oakham, Rutlandshire, where his father, a butcher, kept bulls for George Villiers, the first Duke of Buckingham. When Jeffrey was eight years old, and 18 inches high, he was taken under the Duchess of Buckingham's protection.

It seems to have been a popular pastime of the English to pop little people into pies, and Jeffrey was an ideal size for this sort of thing. When Queen Henrietta Maria came to visit the Duchess at Burleigh-on-the-Hill, shortly after marrying King Charles in 1825, a cold pie was brought to the table, opened with care, and out jumped little Jeffrey.

The Queen was so delighted with his manners and appearance (William Fuller, in his *Worthies of England*, describes Hudson as "without any deformity, wholly proportionable") that the Duchess promptly presented him to the royal visitor.

From all accounts he quickly became a pet of everyone at court with the possible exception of William Evans, the King's huge porter, whom Jeffrey constantly teased. Evans, however, is said to have saved Hudson from being blown into the Thames one day as he clung desperately to a bush during a strong wind.

Jeffrey also found a friend in another of

the Queen's dwarfs, Richard Gibson, who was only four years older than Hudson.

As the years passed, Jeffrey was given a larger role at court than simply that of amusing his royal mistress. Henrietta was the daughter of King Henry IV of France, who was assassinated six months after her birth. When she became pregnant in 1830, Hudson was sent to France to obtain a midwife.

On the return trip the party, which also included the Queen's dancing master, was captured by a Flemish pirate and taken to Dunkirk. Their captor seized valuable gifts from Henrietta's mother, Marie de' Medici, and also was paid a heavy ransom. The mission is said to have cost Hudson about 2,500 English pounds.

Hudson, sometimes known as "Strenuous Jeffrey," was tiny but hot-tempered and seemingly ready for any adventure. He was at Breda during the siege by the Prince of Orange in 1637, apparently having volunteered his services with other Englishmen, including the Earl of Warwick and Earl of Northhampton. And he accompanied the Queen when she fled to France in exile in 1644.

It was at Paris, about 1649, that Hudson quarreled, for some unknown reason, with a Mr. Crofts, brother of Lord Crofts, a member of the Queen's entourage. According to Fuller in his *Worthies of England*, Hudson was, "though a dwarf, no dastard." He challenged Crofts to a duel, and when his opponent showed up armed only with a squirt (a kind of syringe) was so enraged that he renewed the challenge. This time pistols were specified, and Hudson shot and killed Crofts.

Only the intervention of Henrietta Maria kept Hudson out of prison. He was forced to flee France, however, and while at sea was again taken by pirates, this time Turkish. Then the story grows vague. Jeffrey was sold into slavery in Barbary, apparently ransomed by friends, and it is known that he was back in England within ten years, taller by 21 inches, the result, he said, of his ordeal.

After the Restoration, Hudson was given a modest pension by the Duke of Buckingham and other old friends. But trouble still pursued him. In 1679, when he was sixty years old, he was thrown into prison on suspicion of being involved in the fictitious Popish Plot, invented by Titus Oates. He was freed shortly afterward, given small sums by Charles II, and died in 1682.

There is no doubt of the weight of Hudson's reputation. Daniel Mytens, the Flemish artist who was a court painter, did Jeffrey's portrait, and Sir Anthony Vandycke, another Flemish painter, who was knighted by Charles I, did an oil of Hudson with Henrietta Maria.

He also sat for other artists, had a book, *The Newe Yeere's Gift*, dedicated to him in 1636, and in 1638 William D'Avenant published a comic poem, "Jeffreidos," a satirical account of Hudson's first meeting with the pirates.

The Dictionary of National Biography, published in England, ends a long account of Hudson's life thus: "Hudson's waistcoat, breeches, and stockings are in the Ashmolean Museum, Oxford."

Another little person who had—for a short span—a life of incredible daring and danger was a Frenchman named Richebourg, whose obituary ran in *The Times* in 1858 when he died in the St. Germain section of Paris. While reports of his age (eighty or ninety) and his height (23½ inches or 33½) vary, it is agreed that when Richebourg was in the retinue of the Duchesse d'Orléans, mother of the French King, Louis-Philippe, the little man was used to smuggle dispatches past the enemy during the first revolution. The device was simple: Richebourg, dressed in a baby's outfit, was carried by a nursemaid with the papers concealed in his clothing.

The Times story said that Richebourg lived on a pension of three thousand francs a year, given by the Orléans family, and that "he had a great repugnance to strangers, and was alarmed when he heard the

Unknown little person. (Courtesy Gulf Coast Photographic Gallery)

The Prince Imperial of France. (Steel engraving from a photo.)

voice of one; but in his own family he was very lively and cheerful . . . ''

A number of prominent churchmen have been diminutive in size. Among them are Gregory of Tours, born about 538, who became a Frankish historian. Gregory, scion of a prominent Roman family, recovered from a serious childhood illness after a pilgrimage to the tomb of St. Martin of Tours and, in consequence, entered the church. He died in 594, but his *Historia Francorum* is still regarded as the most important source for scholars studying the Franks.

A grandnephew of Roger Bacon, John Baconthorpe, a Carmelite, known as "the resolute doctor," belongs in the same small category. He died in 1346. He was a scholar who "anticipated Wycliffe's teaching that priests should be subordinate to kings."

The diplomatic ranks also were enlivened by the presence, over centuries, of several persons whose size was no clue to their intellectual gifts. A very small Englishman, one Mr. Ramus, was with the British ambassador on a trip to Vienna in the 1670s where, according to the diarist John Evelyn, he spoke so brilliantly in Latin that he was honored by the Viennese Emperor. Another linguist of note was among the aides to the Duke of Parma a century earlier, although only about 36 inches high. He was John de Estrix, a Belgian. And even as early as the twelfth century, Saladin, the enlightened ruler of Egypt and Syria, is said to have had among his ministers the pocket-size Characus, who was less than 48 inches in height.

One of the sights of ancient Rome, too, must have been Gaius Licinius Calvus, who lived from 82 to 47 B.C., and who had to stand on a mound of earth while addressing his fellows. He is said to have been a friend of Gaius Valerius Catullus, the great lyric poet.

A comparable spectacle for the nineteenth-century Londoner was the 36-inch messenger of the House of Parliament, George Trout, who served in that post from 1830 to 1850. Trout once was given 10 pounds by the chief surgeon of one of London's great hospitals for the privilege of performing a postmortem after Trout's death. But the midget outlived the medic. Trout died in 1851 at the age of seventy-six.

There have been warlike little people, too, in addition to Jeffrey Hudson. Garibaldi is said to have had a little volunteer slain during his fight to unite Italy, and at least three Civil War soldiers are reported to have been of very small size. The 192d Ohio boasted of one enlisted man 40 inches tall; the 128th Indiana reported a soldier 49 inches high; and the smallest in

On top: Pygmy and British officer. Below, small soldier from the Boer War, on exhibit at the St. Louis Exposition.

Mike and Ike Matina (Later Mike and Ike Candy, when candy was named for them)
at 1933–34 Century of Progress Exposition, Chicago.

any unit is said to have been 39 inches in height.

But the smallest-soldier honor seems to belong to an Englishman, later exhibited at the St. Louis Exposition, who reportedly was less than 3 feet tall, yet fought for the British during the Boer War.

Those who couldn't fight in later wars, when the military was less flexible, did their part in other ways. Prince Paul, for example, one of the clowns now with Ringling Bros. and Barnum & Bailey, was a welder in an East Coast shipyard during World War II; Mike and Ike Matina (re-

Mike and Ike take on World Welterweight champ, Jackie Fields.

member the phrase "Mike and Ike, they look alike"?) sold war bonds during New York City street rallies in the World War I days; and many men and women whose small size kept them out of uniform were indispensable in World War II factories and shipyards.

A large group of little persons was honored by President Franklin D. Roosevelt at Ypsilanti, Michigan, for their outstanding efforts in aircraft construction. Similar work was done in West Coast airplane plants and in navy yards such as that at Norfolk, Virginia, where small workers were of great value.

Final modern-warfare note: News reports in 1977 stated that pygmies, armed with poison darts, were aiding Zaire in its battle with Angola.

Final royal little person note: The Duke of Altamira, who lived in Spain, was known to the populace as the Little King (Rey Chico) and was described in 1856 by Lord Hollander as "the least man I ever saw in society and smaller than many dwarfs exhibited for money."

Mike (or Ike) with Lilliputian trouper. (Pach Bros. Photo, N.Y.C.)

Grace and Harry Doll.

The Little Prodigies

QUEEN HENRIETTA MARIA, wife of King Charles I of England, once played matchmaker. Whether she did so out of idle curiosity, which queens can afford to indulge, or some innate kindness, it is impossible to determine.

Whatever the reason, the marriage of Richard Gibson, one of the court painters, to Anne Shepherd, a member of Her Majesty's retinue, came about at Queen Henrietta Maria's suggestion. While no one could say the match was made in heaven, it seems safe to assume that no one went around saying it wasn't made there, either. The couple seemed ideally suited to each other.

Gibson was personable and an excellent artist. He studied under Sir Peter Lely, the Dutch painter, who came to the English court in 1641. The bride was charming and beautiful and exactly as tall as her husband—3 feet 10 inches.

Everyone who was anyone turned out for the ceremony at Hampton Court, where some of Gibson's portrait miniatures still hang. King Charles gave the bride away, and Queen Henrietta Maria presented her with a diamond ring. There were toasts and much gaiety, and Edmund Waller, the noted poet, immortalized the affair in a rhymed tribute called "Of the Marriage of the Dwarfs," which began:

Design, or chance, makes others wive;
But Nature did this match contrive . . .

Gibson was born in Cumberland in 1615. A kind and wealthy woman, whose page he was, noticed his artistic ability and persuaded Francis Cleyne, or De Clein, to give him instruction. Cleyne was in charge of the tapestry works at Mortlake, where the royal tapestries were fashioned.

Gibson soon came to court as backstairs page for the King, and became drawing master to Mary and Anne, daughters of the future James II, when they were young. He must have pleased them, because when Mary wed William of Orange in 1677, she took Gibson along to Holland for a considerable period.

The command-performance marriage turned out very well for the Gibsons. They had nine children, five of whom lived to adulthood. All were of normal size. Gibson died on July 23, 1690, at the age of seventy-five. Anne, who was five years younger, outlived him by nineteen years. Several paintings of the couple survive, among them one by Vandycke showing Anne with the Duchess of Windsor, and Lely's hand-in-hand portrait of both.

There was a well-known German painter, Jacob Lehnen, a little person, who never achieved the fame accorded Gibson, and some two centuries after the English painter died, Charles Ludwig, who was to become known professionally as Prince Ludwig, the smallest artist in the world, was born in Thuringen, Saxony.

The Prince, who had two brothers killed in World War I, was 34 inches tall and weighed 32 pounds at the age of twenty. One of his mother's sisters was also diminutive. Ludwig and his wife, Elizabeth Hoy, another small person, appeared at the Century of Progress Exposition in Chicago in 1933.

The engagement cannot have been a very profitable one. Elizabeth Hoy died in the Cook County Hospital charity ward after the fair ended, and about forty of her little friends took up a collection to bury her in a plot donated by one of their number. The gesture seems to have been an unhesitating one, even though, like Ludwig, they were virtually stranded and almost without funds.

Prince Ludwig appeared a year later at the International Exposition in San Diego, and in 1938 played in the movie version of *The Wizard of Oz.*

A Russian artist named Ratoucheff, who formed his own little people troupe and toured with European circuses, studied in Paris for many years and had a one-man show there in 1930. The group lived in a chateau near Paris during the off season, but their subsequent history after the coming of the Nazis is unclear.

The list of little musicians is long and talent-laden. During the eighteenth century Romando, a native of Portugal, was noted for his ability to imitate various musical instruments and animal sounds with incredible skill, using only his voice.

Another eighteenth-century figure, or half-figure, Marco Catozze, was proficient on the drums despite having neither arms nor legs. He did have hands, but these grew directly from his shoulders.

Buchinger, another terribly deformed little person, has been described at some length earlier, but deserves mention here as well, since he was a master of the flute, bagpipe, and trumpet.

Late in the nineteenth century, an Austrian pianist, Nannette Stocker, who was 33 inches tall and weighed 33 pounds, began giving recitals. When she was sixteen years old, and appearing in Strasbourg, she met John Hauptman, a fine violinist, who was only three inches taller. Eventually the two began appearing together. After some years of successful European engagements, they came to London in March 1815, where they were enthusiastically received.

According to a writer who saw them at that time, Nannette was lively and smiling, Hauptman slow-moving and withdrawn, perhaps—or so the story goes—because he had proposed marriage to his partner and been turned down.

The United States had many midget musicians during the latter part of the nineteenth century. Rosie Wolff, the German Rose, appeared with her violin in many dime museums in the 1870s, and Herman Rice and his sisters, Augusta and Anne, also played on the same circuit. Major and Fanny Burdett, and General Gardenus, were seen in 1884 at Drerr's Dance Museum in Chicago.

Others with musical talent were Bertha Cunningham (or Carihan), the Lilliputian Princess from Minnesota, who was with Ringling Brothers Circus from 1886 to

Prince Ludwig admires his work.

Singer's famous troupe.

1892; Corita the Doll Lady; the Count and Countess DeKay; Eva Evalina; Great Peter the Small; and Casper Weis, leader of a little people band that was on the road with Barnum and Bailey in 1883.

The twentieth century also has heard the sound of music from many gifted little people. There were groups such as Leo Singer's Midgets, for which he used to hunt the world for recruits; Bob Hermine's Midget Group, also active in the twenties and thirties; Midget Joe, a xylophonist with Cole Brothers Circus in the later twenties who often appeared with the Fisher Giants. And there was Pee Wee Marquette, master of ceremonies at the New Zanzibar Café on Broadway, who sang and did routines with the big-name bands booked into that club.

The Spike Jones band, one of the zaniest groups ever put together, wouldn't have been complete during the forties without the help of that talented small person Billy Barty, who later founded the Little People of America.

Many of the musicians mentioned, among them Barty, also had (or have) acting ability to a marked degree. One of the earliest little people with a gift for dramatics was John Coan, born in Norfolk, England, in 1728, who was 3 feet high and weighed 27½ pounds at the age of sixteen.

While appearing in London "at the Watchmakers, facing the Cannon Tavern, Charing Cross," Coan was presented to the royal family and won much attention in consequence. He is said to have written a poem honoring the Prince of Wales, which he recited at the Prince's birthday party.

Coan, who was fond of giving dramatic recitations, appeared in a play called *Fine Gentlemen in Lethe* at Tunbridge Wells, and toward the end of his career was exhibited with Edward Bamford, a London hatter, whose 7 feet 4 inches gave him giant stature in those shorter days. Coan died in 1764, while serving as a kind of greeter at the Dwarf's Tavern in Chelsea Fields, where his effigy was then placed on display.

There have been at least two undersize magicians, Joseph Zaino, born on April 12, 1877, who was 42 inches high, and Colonel Charles, who also was a wire-walker and singer. Colonel Charles appeared in a Dreamland sideshow from 1904 until fire destroyed the amusement complex in 1907, and traveled with Barnum and Bailey for many years.

Another eighteenth-century British actor was Bobby Ralston, who was with a tent circus in England, and became famous in his role as the wolf in *Little Red Riding Hood.*

Back across the Atlantic, one of the most dapper figures on Broadway about fifty years ago was Little Lord Roberts, known to the frequenters of the Great White Way simply as Bobs. Little Lord Roberts, always dressed in the latest fashion and with a very large cigar clenched between tiny teeth, is said to have made $750 weekly before the stock market crash wiped out his paper fortune along with that of thousands of others.

Among the most graceful of the female little people was Dolly Dutton, a nineteenth-century ballet dancer, singer, and comedienne, who with her sister was appearing during the Civil War as the Little Fairies. Dollie was born in Farmington, Massachusetts, in 1856. When a "grown-up," she weighed only 13 pounds and was 26 inches tall.

Another feminine performer was Jeanne Weis, a comedienne, who was born in Paris on August 31, 1883. She did a vaudeville skit in which she headed a gangster outfit, and while playing at Dreamland on Coney Island met and married Casper Weis, the bandleader. Jeanne was 38 inches tall and weighed 45 pounds.

From left, Eva Evaline. (C. A. Henkel Photo, N.Y.C.) Dolly Dunton, and General Gardenus.

Rosie Wolff, the German Rose, a gifted violinist, as seen by Eisenmann and on far right by Casilly of St. Louis.

One of the best-known families of little people consisted of Harry Doll, born Kurt Schneider, and his sisters, Grace, Daisy, and Tiny. Kurt and Grace were the first to reach this country from their native Germany. They danced at Luna Park as the Earles. When the two younger sisters arrived, the Doll name was adopted. The four were with the Ringling Brothers Circus for many years. In 1925 Harry starred in a Lon Chaney motion picture, *The Unholy Three.* In the film Harry, dressed as a baby, aided three thieves to commit burglaries after they boosted him through various transoms.

Harry and Daisy also appeared in the controversial Tod Browning film, *Freaks,* which was attacked by various little people.

Augusta, Herman and Anne Rice (Henkel, N.Y.C.): Augusta and Herman in much later view; Augusta and Herman in Eisenmann's studio.

Captain Liable appearing in play "Love of Livery or Irish Perseverence." The taller people in the photograph are an acting team, the Brennans c. 1880.

In 1939 the Del Rios were sued by their manager, Jack Tavlin, who took them to court for allegedly failing to live up to the terms of their contract: They refused to sell picture postcards of themselves on Sunday, or, indeed, to work at all on that day. Unhappily, the court ruling was in Tavlin's favor.

Finally, what better person could you find as the top lawman for the Midget Village at the 1933 Chicago Fair than Thomas J. Keenan, who campaigned for the election as chief of police by announcing that he was not only the greatest comedian of all time but also a doctor, an electrician, and a champion prizefighter— at any weight!

He anticipated the Little People of America motto—"Think Big" by almost twenty-five years.

groups and others as offensive. The Dolls were in several other pictures as well, including *The Wizard of Oz* with Judy Garland and a marquee full of top-drawer stars.

Harry's role in *The Unholy Three* recalls the real-life part played by Runi Tober, a nineteenth-century Italian man of very small stature, who, the *Enciclopedia dello Spettacolo* tells us, was carried in a suitcase by fellow burglars to be smuggled into places they planned to loot.

Another family group, working out of Chicago, was the Del Rios; Paul, Trinidad, and Delores, whose genuine family name was Rodriguez. They played such spots as Mamid's Million-Dollar Pier in Atlantic City, and also were in demand for opening-day ceremonies at Chicago department stores and other pedestrian chores.

Top left: King Rector, 23 years old; 42 inches tall, 45 pounds. Top right: Robert Delgavin, also known as Lord Robert or simply Bobs, a boulevardier. At bottom left Prince Harry, to the right Princess Tiny.

#51

GRACE

The Doll Family, one of the best known of little people groups; also known earlier as the Earles.

Pee Wee Marquette, entertainer at New York City's Zanzibar Cafe during the 1940's. (United Press International Photo)

Rossow's Midgets.
(Charles King Coll.)

The Writers, People in Advertising, and the Athletes

ONLY WHEN SOME TASK depends upon normal human size is a little person handicapped. Anything the average person can do with his *mind* also can be accomplished by those who may be two or three feet shorter.

Alypius of Alexandria, who probably was born near the middle of the fourth century, was said by contemporary historians to have been no more than 18 inches tall. While this figure may be viewed with some skepticism, it seems certain he was far below usual height. But Alypius was a noted writer about music, whose *Introduction to Music,* to quote the *Encyclopaedia Britannica,* "describes the 15 transcriptions of the scale in vocal and instrumental music in the diatomic and chromatic systems, and nine transpositions in the enharmonic system, with tables of their notation."

Playwright? William Gabriel, who for years was known for his portrayal of Buster Brown, decided to write, star in, and produce a play. He raised money by selling the family farm in Rhode Island and wrote

a play called *Solitaire.* The drama failed, and Gabriel died in 1931, possibly of a broken heart. But what taller playwrights haven't also failed?

Newspaper editor? A. L. Sawyer edited the popular and highly regarded *Democrat* in Florida during the 1880s.

Newspaper reporter? Daniel Y. McMullen was a Chicago newspaperman around the turn of the century. He later became a banker in a small town in Illinois.

Golfer? A European player of small physical stature named Gabor Bagi is described as having been very good indeed.

A man named George Warren Brown was responsible for a number of employment opportunities for small persons. Brown founded the Buster Brown Shoe Company, the trademark for which was a little boy with his dog, Tige.

In 1904 the firm hired the first of what became a series of little people, the first one William H. Ray, of Hornersville, Missouri, who had been with Barnum and Bailey and Sells Bros. circuses, and worked on the

Golden City, a showboat owned by William H. Stowes. Ray, whose professional name was Major Willis, remained with the Buster Brown Company until 1915 when they quit sending a variety of little persons with a variety of Tiges to department stores, theaters, and shoe stores.

When Ray was married in 1926, at the age of sixty-six, virtually everyone in Hornersville turned out for the nuptials.

Another of the many Buster Browns was Johnny Clifton, who must have become very tired of chanting the ritual:

I'm Buster Brown, I live in a shoe.
That's my dog Tige, he lives there too.

Clifton and his wife, Selecta, also a little person, opened a sandwich shop in Austin, Texas, in 1925. It was called, naturally, the Buster Brown Sandwich Shop. Clifton died in Austin in 1978. He was eighty-nine years old and had entertained thousands of youngsters, wearing his Little Lord Fauntleroy coat, with knickers, a red beret, and a blond wig.

Clifton's favorite Tige was a bulldog, which wore eyeglasses and held a pipe in its mouth. It may be difficult for you to believe, but it is claimed that on command from Clifton, Tige would waddle into an audience of children, find some spectator who was not wearing Buster Brown shoes, and gently try to remove the offending footgear with his teeth.

The Cliftons had one daughter, also tiny, whose name was Myrna. She married a suitably small husband, Clarence Swenson, who later appeared in *The Wizard of Oz*. The Swensons had two mini-daughters, a third-generation phenomenon which appears to be unmatched.

*Johnny Clifton and Tige. He was the second in a series of
Buster Browns. (Courtesy of Brown Shoe Co.)*

A number of other little people played Buster Brown, among them Major Jack Fox, A. J. Rosemondo, Dick Barker, Jack and Herbert Barnett, brothers, whose side-show names were King Jack Barnett and Cap†ain Herbert Barnett, the latter also known as Dainty Demdrops and Admiral Thumb. He was 42 inches tall.

Capt. Jack Barnett (left) and son, Herbert, also known as Admiral Thumb and Dainty Demdrops. (Photo by Wendt, Boonton, N.J.)

King Jack, who was married to Dorothy Warfield, a full-size woman, was 39 inches tall.

Probably the most famous of all modern advertising little folk was Johnny Roventino, who was a New York City bellhop in 1932 when an advertising agency man heard him paging and asked him to transfer his talents to Phillip Morris, one of the agency's customers. Roventino, who was 20 years old and 47 inches high at the time, was signed to a contract at $20,000 a year, and remained the highly distinctive voice of Phillip Morris for many years.

A great many firms employed little spokesmen for their products, including the Hiram Walker company, who found Captain Werner Ritter, a native of Germany and certainly one of the most diminutive symbols of all time. Ritter, at twenty-one, weighed just under 20 pounds and was 18 inches tall. When working at the Hiram Walker exhibit at the 1933 Chicago Fair, he was termed the Pint-Sized Sweetheart of Midget Village. Werner was a member of the Emil Ritter Midgets during the 1920s and '30s.

If you're ever prowling your favorite flea market, you may (as did the authors) run across a card or candy tray bearing the photograph of Mr. and Mrs. Jean Bregant, who represented the Woodward Candy Company, an Iowa concern. The Bregants also played the World's Fair and Trade Exposition circuits.

Early Times promoted its whiskey through the medium of a little person known, by odd coincidence, as Earle E. Times, who was said to be one of the world's strongest men, pound for pound, with the ability to lift four full-size adults at the same time.

Other small advertising persons included Helen Haskell, who played fairs and business shows, often around Detroit, from 1907 to 1933; Mr. and Mrs. N. G. Winner, well-known vaudeville, dime-museum, and circus performers, whose romance was publicized in *White Tops,* a circus magazine, in an item stating that Winner was corresponding with "a little Michigan lady" and that his intentions were serious.

Sometimes the names have been forgotten. The Sunshine Baking Company had one of its trade-fair booths in the 1930s run by a seven-person team of little folk. Bowman Dairy, a Chicago concern, had Bud and Betty Bowman on their payroll, and the Oscar Mayer Packing Company, in Chicago at least, dramatized their products by means of a small man in chef's costume driving a car shaped like a hot dog through the city streets.

Capt. Ritter, shown at the Hiram Walker display, 1933–34 Century of Progress Exposition, Chicago. (Circus World Museum, N.J.)

There have always been little people with big athletic talent, including the previously mentioned Polander Dwarf, a horseback rider with the Rickett's Circus.

Another fine rider was Harvey Leech, a native of Westchester, New York, who also was known as Hervio Nano and the Gnome Fly. In addition to his acting skills, he is said to have been able to leap from the ground to the back of a moving horse and to have been one to avoid in a free-for-all, since he possessed a punch out of all proportion to his size. Leech was known on both sides of the Atlantic, and Barnum is said to have tried to sign him for his museum, with plans to bill him as the Wild Man of the Prairies.

Master Tony Lowande, who was older than he seemed, was a competent acrobat in the 1860s, as were the Siegrist Midgets, whose billing was the Acrobatic Marvels, seen in the Chicago Coliseum in the 1870s. Another famous duo was Mike and Ike Matina, who are believed to have worked earlier, with Herman Rossow, as the Rossow Midgets. The two were competent boxers, wrestlers, weight lifters, and acrobats. Then there were the Piccolo Midgets, who included Baron Paucci, and specialized in comedy, boxing exhibitions, and acrobatic work, and others:

Shorty Healy, gymnast and comic, who, with his full-size partner, were known as Spontaneous Combustion; Gulliver's Lilliputians, who appeared with Barnum and Bailey from 1900 to 1907, and boasted of a spectacular trio: Princess Isabella sang and danced, Prince Louis was an acrobat, and Prince Charles was a magician and wire-walker.

Emil Ritter's Midgets (below); *with alligator,* (top).

Mr. and Mrs. N. G. Winner on tour in Marietta, O.

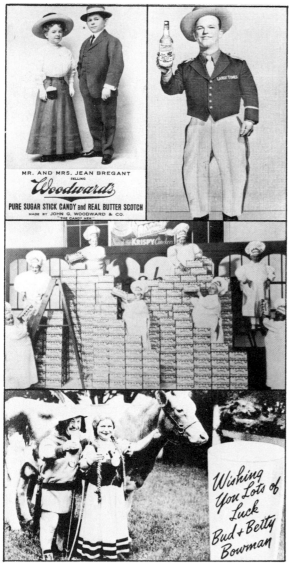

MR. AND MRS. JEAN BREGANT
SELLING
Woodward's
PURE SUGAR STICK CANDY and REAL BUTTER SCOTCH
MADE BY JOHN G. WOODWARD & CO.
THE CANDY MEN

Wishing You Lots of Luck Bud + Betty Bowman

*The Bregants (above left) on advertising card and (right)
Earl E. Times for Early Times. Bud and Betty Bowman,
center, and Sunshine's little people, below.*

The Princess Mariska, an excellent athlete, should be mentioned also, as should Count Phillipe Nichole and his wife, the Countess Nichole. The Count was a circus strong man and weight lifter, born in the Province of Quebec, September 27, 1881. His wife, Rose Dufresne, born in Quebec province about six years later, toured with Phillipe after their marriage in 1906. The couple eventually opened a museum in their home in Montreal, where they sold souvenirs, which included chinaware bearing their pictures. They had one son, small, C. N. Nichole, Jr.

Wrestling is the one sport in which the little person has been able to make a considerable sum of money. Gay Talese, in a *New York Times* story in 1958, described a troupe of midget wrestlers who included Tito Infanti, Farmer McGregor, Pee Wee James, Fuzzy Cupid, Lord Littlebrook, Cowboy Bradley, Little Beaver, Sky Low, who reportedly could lift 460 pounds, and Major Tom Thumb, a former circus strong man. Members of the group traveled in a Cadillac, which seated eight midgets and the normal-size driver, and Talese reported that the 93-pound Tito earned as much as $70,000 yearly.

Twenty years later midget wrestling still was popular. A Chicago program that also included women wrestlers and full-size male wrestlers offered Wee Willie and Mighty Cupid, who knew all the tricks, both physical and acting ones, and were what all promoters look for: crowd pleasers.

To become international again, mention should be made of Harold Simmons, now almost sixty, who still does acrobatic work at Shrine Circuses and other places. He is a native of Australia, where he was spotted and signed as a youngster while doing acrobatic feats at the beach. Since then the 4-foot 4-inch Simmons has visited Europe and Africa but now lives in Sarasota, Florida, during the off season (about two months). He worked in an assembly plant in Adelaide during World War II, and mentioned, after having appeared on Bozo's Circus at WGN-TV Chicago, that he no longer drinks.

"Gene Randow, a clown with whom I used to work," said Simmons, smiling merrily, "used to say: 'When Harold gets a few drinks he thinks he's ten feet tall.' I'd take on the world."

Now we come to a small person who achieved world fame in a matter of perhaps five minutes, all because of a kind of modern-day Barnum, touched with compassion and a lot of class, named Bill Veeck. At the time, Veeck was boss of a downtrodden but never dull baseball team, the St. Louis Browns.

The small person was Eddie Gaedel, a Chicagoan, who was hired by Veeck for a single afternoon's work during the 1951 season. But Veeck tells it best:

"It came about in a kind of strange way. We were in St. Louis hustling customers. Our sponsors were Falstaff, and we conceived the idea of getting Falstaff to get all their distributors and to have the distributors, in turn, get all their customers, to come to the ball park for a Falstaff family party. As part of selling Falstaff on the idea, I promised them to do something that nobody had ever seen before and that would stir up a great deal of conversation;

that everybody who came would find this to be a memorable afternoon.

"At the time I didn't know what it would be, but I figured I'd think of something. And that's why I had to keep it secret, because—I told them—well, if I tell you then it won't be a secret anymore. But of course the reason I didn't tell them is because *I* didn't know what it was. So then I got to thinking as the time came closer for this thing, and it occurred to me one morning—I was sitting in the bathtub soaking my legs, which I do every morning, which is when most of my ideas, good, bad, or indifferent, occur—that years before when I was a youngster my daddy was a very good friend of John McGraw's.

Two more advertising men, Bill and Jack.

"In those days, instead of a bat boy, they had a mascot. John McGraw's mascot was a hunchback of very small stature, and the Giants were very good in those days and the Cubs were very bad. This is in the early twenties. My daddy would bring John McGraw out to the house for dinner, and McGraw would always threaten that he was going to use Mitimaro, or whatever his name was, I can't remember his name really—the Cubs were so bad he was going to put him up to bat. The crowning insult, you know, to how bad the Cubs were.

"This was very funny to me. It wasn't to my daddy, but it was to me. I remembered this, and I thought: This isn't so bad, and this is where the Eddie Gaedel idea came from. So I called Marty Caine, the booking agent, in Cleveland and said: 'Will you get

*Two Rossow Midgets square off (Photo by Hall, N.Y.C.) and (Inset) Rossow and
two little people. (Charles King Coll.)*

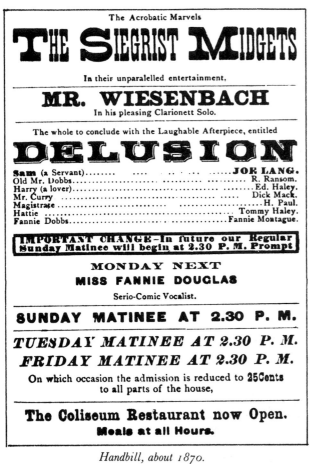

The Acrobatic Marvels

THE SIEGRIST MIDGETS

In their unparalelled entertainment,

MR. WIESENBACH

In his pleasing Clarionett Solo.

The whole to conclude with the Laughable Afterpiece, entitled

DELUSION

Sam (a Servant)........ ... ...JOE LANG.
Old Mr. Dobbs............................... ....R. Ransom.
Harry (a lover)....................................Ed. Haley.
Mr. Curry ....Dick Mack.
Magistrate..H. Paul.
Hattie .... Tommy Haley.
Fannie Dobbs............................Fannie Montague.

IMPORTANT CHANGE—In future our Regular
Sunday Matinee will begin at 2.30 P. M. Prompt

MONDAY NEXT
MISS FANNIE DOUGLAS

Serio-Comic Vocalist.

SUNDAY MATINEE AT 2.30 P. M.

TUESDAY MATINEE AT 2.30 P. M.
FRIDAY MATINEE AT 2.30 P. M.

On which occasion the admission is reduced to 25 Cents
to all parts of the house,

The Coliseum Restaurant now Open.
Meals at all Hours.

Handbill, about 1870.

me a small man who has some courage.' "

The agent suggested Gaedel, whom Veeck then signed to a one-day contract. His next step was to bring Gaedel to St. Louis and give him coaching on how to stand at the plate.

"The interesting thing is we had a perfect stance for him, with crouching, so that he had *no* strike zone, which was the point I was going to make with the whole thing— that the rules are so strangely written sometimes. Because when he crouched, and dropped his shoulders, he had no strike zone at all! But he spread out; he'd seen DiMaggio too often. So we gave him an inch-and-a-half strike zone.

"The funny part of this thing is that I had this cake, finally, and we got Eddie into it and wheeled it out before the game, and Sir Falstaff came down, dressed in his Elizabethan outfit, and opened the cake and Eddie stepped out.

"The people from Falstaff and the advertising agency said: 'This is great? This is a gag you've used before. There's nothing sensational about this.' So when they opened the cake and the little guy stepped out they all said: 'That's not so funny. That's not much.' And they fled. All of a sudden I'm all alone. Nobody's going to be associated with—you know—this disaster . . .

"Now when he walks to the plate during the game, which had never occurred to them—that I might have the temerity to use him as a player with the l/8th on his back, all of a sudden I'm a hero again and they all come back: 'What a wonderful idea!' That shows you about advertising agencies.

"The crowd reaction was first disbelief, then laughter. The umpire, Eddie Hurley, went over to the bench to make sure this was legitimate. Of course we had him signed to a contract and had notified the league office. So there was nothing he could do about it.

The Siegrist Midgets, with Tony Lowande on the left. (Photo by Drew and Maxwell, N.Y.C.)

*Master Tony Lowande,
Acrobatic star of Sie-
grist's Midgets. by
Wilkes, Baltimore,
Md., c. 1860.)*

"Bob Swift, the Detroit catcher, started to lie down behind the plate to give the pitcher, Bobby Cain, a fair target. But Hurley thought this destroyed the dignity of the game and ordered him up. So Swift got down on both knees. Bobby Cain tried on his first two pitches to get the ball over but he missed by a foot. By this time he's laughing so hard the next two became automatic.

"Gaedel had a Hillerich and Bradsby miniature bat, which he handled quite nicely, but the one thing I told him was: 'Look, don't swing! If you swing, I'm going to be sitting in the press box with a rifle and I'll shoot you right in the head.' He wasn't sure whether I would or not, nor am I. When he walked we sent in a runner for him, but not before he had his moment of glory, standing on the bag and taking a lead.

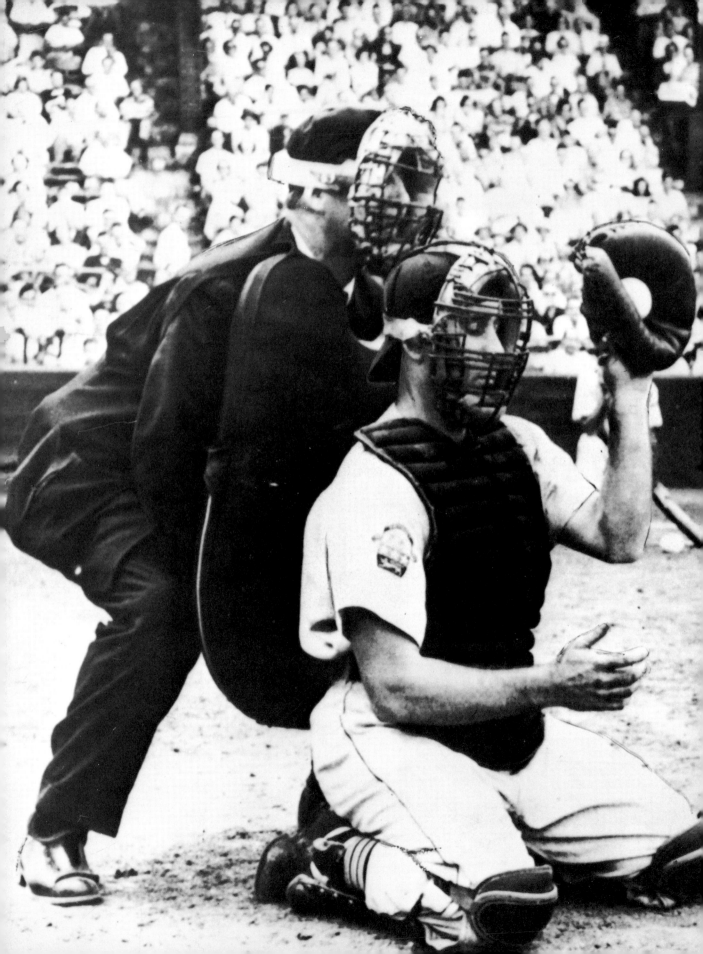

Eddie Gaedel enters baseball's Hall of Fame. (St. Louis Post-Dispatch Photo.)

"Meanwhile, Will Harridge, the league president, was calling the park to reprimand me, I suppose—I don't know what he really had in mind—for making a travesty out of the game. That was always the line they used with me: 'You're making a travesty out of the game!' So I told Ada Ireland: 'Look, just close the board. No use letting him scream.' All over the country people were calling, saying what a terrible thing I had done by holding the entire national pastime up to ridicule.

"Actually, an interesting thing—we had about 24,000 at the ball park, a very large crowd for the Brownies. But now, in retrospect, in order just to pick out the people I talked with who were there, our capacity had to be about 240,000. It's kind of like all those people who came over on the *Mayflower*. It would take eight *Queen Marys* dragging behind, 200, you know, rafts filled with people to get all those people who came over on the *Mayflower*.

"People saw the unveiling of Eddie Gaedel in Cleveland; they saw it in Detroit. It was seen all over. One of the strange aftermaths was that the teams around the league heard about this, and in those days you traveled by Pullman car instead of flying. So they're all practicing in the aisles to see how you handle an inch-and-a-half strike zone. But I had no intention of using him again. I made my point, discharged my obligation to Falstaff, and stuck a few pins in a few stuffed shirts and enjoyed it."

Veeck said that Gaedel also had a good time, after he got over a brief attack of stage fright.

"He didn't turn reluctant until it came right down to getting into the cake, then he began to get cold feet. Our traveling secretary, Bill Durney, who was about six feet four and weighed around three hundred pounds, said: 'Look, into the cake! Or there won't be enough of you left to make a candle.'

"It really was fun, and would there were more occasions like this when there wasn't anything you could lose. We were going to

finish seventh and Detroit eighth no matter what happened. It couldn't make the slightest difference to the standings, and yet it seemed, like now, that the slightest bit of levity was out of place in what has become a grim and serious affair. Eddie Gaedel certainly tried harder than anybody else on our team. He got on base, and that's something very few of our athletes could claim."

There were rulings from the league office, of course. Harridge announced that no more midgets would be allowed to play, and that Gaedel's time at bat would be officially ignored and omitted from the record books. Veeck demolished both decisions with his own brand of logic.

"I wrote back to Harridge: 'Fine, let's establish what is a midget in fact. Is it three feet six inches, Eddie's height? Is it four feet six? If it's five feet six, that's great. We can get rid of Rizzuto.' And I pointed out that they couldn't balance the books if they didn't put Gaedel in. Somehow they had to account for his being on first base, and someone running for him, and the extra walk Bobby Cain had given. So they let him in.

"You know if I'd had any courage, and we'd used eight other fellows like Eddie, we might have won a game or so. We'd have run around and around and around and might never have *finished* the game."

Veeck then pointed out that as he was talking the White Sox had at shortstop the smallest fellow, next to Gaedel, who ever played big-league baseball: Harry Chappas, who is five feet three.

"It's not that he's that *little*," Veeck said. "He's that short. He's a very powerful young man, pound for pound and inch for inch. Does that make him a midget, illegal, immoral, or something? No. He can just play better than guys that are a foot taller than he.

"I'll tell you one thing about the little people. If Harry Chappas can play as well as we think he can, he could well turn out to be second only to Reggie Jackson or Mr.

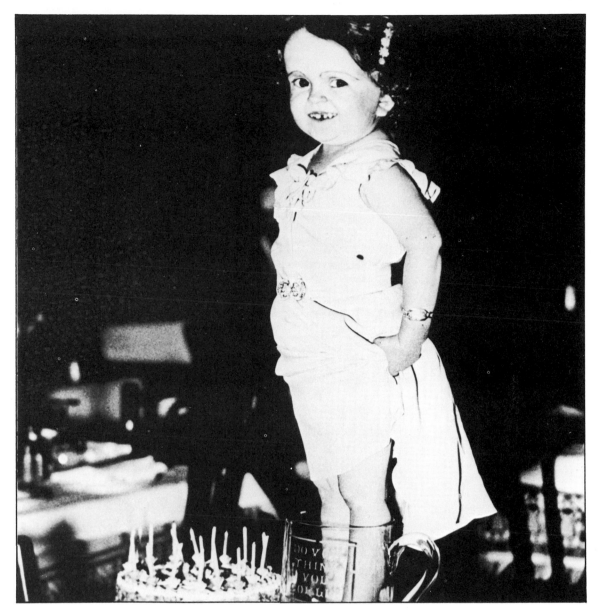

Miss Margaret Ann Robinson, who was only 21 inches high, celebrated her 19th birthday in 1935 with a party at Leon and Eddie's in N.Y.C. (U.P.I. Photo.)

Parker as a drawing card. Because there are more people of short stature than there are giants, even if you wouldn't believe that watching basketball. As a matter of fact one of the things about baseball is that it's the only game left for humans. Because to play basketball you have to be seven feet six, and in order to play football you have to be the same width.

"Here is an interesting thing: If Little David hadn't belted away Big Goliath, you'd never have heard of either of the bums. If Goliath had just scrounged him into the ground, so what? But it's a fact that we all favor the underdog. Fellows who succeed against tremendous odds. The idea that a kid would believe he could play in the majors at five feet three and play well immediately solicits—not sympathy, but support. And it's going to do a great deal for the morale of all people who are less than average height."

Singer's Midgets come to the United States from Vienna. (Photo by Pach Bros., N.Y.C.)

The Show Groups

T̲H̲E̲ ̲ A T T R A C T I O N   T H A T
the little people have held for promoters,
whether of the quick-buck or legitimate
(P. T. Barnum) variety, is many centuries
old. It is not possible to know exactly what
percentage of blandishments, honest or
otherwise, the little people succumbed to.

But a privately printed book of reminis-
cences by William Riddle, *Cherished Memories* (Lancaster, Pa., 1910), relates the story
of one such approach that failed. It con-
cerns a small man identified only as
"Steffy," about 1851.

> Steffy was born and reared somewhere in
> the eastern part of the country. Only four
> feet in height, with body out of all propor-
> tion to the length of his pedal extremities,
> and half-century-old stovepipe hat perched
> on the top of his well-shaped cranium, with
> a long, black stogie between his teeth, our
> prototype could be looked for after each
> important election with the returns securely
> stored away in the crown of his steeple-
> shaped headgear. Stepping into the head-
> quarters of the "Thugs" and spreading out
> the tally-sheet before the coterie of political

> bosses, Steffy stood prepared for any
> changes which might make things solid for
> "Mulhooly," as the saying went.
> Whether this product of the Welsh-
> mountain district had imbibed too much of
> Mishler's Bitters or labels of different qual-
> ity, has escaped our storehouse of
> memory. . . .

*Leo Singer in Midget Village in Vienna, with
two of the troupe.*

The Singer troupe in costume. Inset shows portion of group as they appeared in Vienna.

MOLKEREI LILIPUT,

Singer's Lilliputians. (Photo by Pach Bros., N.Y.C.)

Discussing the Midway to be found each year at the Lancaster County Agricultural Fair, although he calls it the "Museum," Riddle also writes:

> Referring again to the "Museum," we have no recollection of ever having met "Steffy" posing as a "dwarf" or strolling 'round taking in the sights. We have, however a very distinct reminder of having seen Ben Mishler's protege, who, usually when in the city, made his home with the man who built a house in a single day of ten hours.
>
> It's been said that on one occasion Steffy was approached by a showman, who on learning he had passed his century mark, offered him a good round sum to travel with the show as a freak. The bargain having been consummated, Steffy asked time to consult his father before leaving home. "Your father, your father! Why, why, where in thunder is your father?" "Oh, he's upstairs nursing grandfather," came as he started to go his way.

It appears that Steffy was not only an accepted resident of his community but also a person who regarded himself as being normal as anyone else. Happily, some little people have always been able to do this, while others are more at ease with companions of small stature, which may account for the existence of midget villages and a number of famous midget troupes.

One of the most attractive of the midget villages was seen at the Century of Progress Exposition in Chicago, which opened in 1933 and was, or so the World's Fair Guide declared, "a reproduction—reduced to midget scale—of the ancient Bavarian city of Dinkelspuhl, one of the few remaining walled towns in Europe." It had forty-five buildings, its own police and fire departments, a church, school, filling station, newspaper, and souvenir stores.

The little town had sixty or seventy residents of diminutive size, as well as some larger family members. Major Doyle, 33 inches tall, was mayor. Other villagers included Mike and Ike Matina, twin brothers, originally from Hungary. Ike was married to Margaret Nickloy, a little lady, who divorced him before the fair was over.

Mr. and Mrs. Raymond Schultz of Woodside, Long Island, were villagers also. Schultz was a sentry on the town walls, and Mrs. Schultz worked in the ice cream parlor. The couple had two daughters, both of normal stature, three-year-old Anita and five-year-old Dorothy.

The oldest and perhaps best-known of the group was Jennie Quigley, eighty-three years old, who lived in the village hotel.

She had been a Chicago resident since shortly after the Chicago fire of 1871. Another resident of the small hotel was Nona Appleby, known as the American Doll Lady.

The village, admission to which was twenty-five cents, also boasted a theater, where there were stage shows each hour, and a restaurant, where meals were served to the public. A note in the *Weekly* reminds visitors that while everything else in the Midget Village was built to scale for the occupants, "the Midget restaurant serves full size meals."

According to Hersey and Bodin in *The World of Midgets*, half the residents (and

Unknown Mayor of unknown community presents key of city to Singer's troupe. (Jennings Photo)

Singer's little people in formal pose. (Photo by Apeda, N.Y.C., from Circus World Museum, Baraboo, Wis.)

they place the village little people population at seventy-two) were native Americans and another 14 percent naturalized citizens. The others had lived in the United States for many years and "not one midget was imported."

Credit for the exclusion of foreign little persons goes to Major Doyle, the brash Manhattan man-about-town, who was sixty-three when the fair opened. Word had been spread through the ranks of the little people entertainers that Century of Progress authorities planned to bring a group of Europeans to populate Midget Village. This enraged Doyle, who began getting newspaper space by proclaiming his outrage.

Doyle pointed out that native, or at least resident, American mini-entertainers were hard hit by the Depression, and that bringing in overseas talent would be un-American. He spoke to a couple of senators, threatened to take the matter to Washington in an attempt to prevent unfair competition, and, in short, raised such a fuss and obtained so much publicity that the fair promoters capitulated. No imports were allowed.

When the Chicago Fair ended in 1934, Doyle and about thirty of the Midget Villagers packed up and moved to the San Diego International Exposition, which opened in 1935 with both a Midget Village and a Midget Farm. Others of the troupe were stranded in Chicago and broke, at least for a time.

Later, when a call went out for Munchkins to appear with Judy Garland in *The Wizard of Oz*, Doyle is credited with having helped line up little people from everywhere, including abroad, to help ensure the success of that remarkable film.

John Lahr, in his *Notes on a Cowardly Lion*, a fascinating biography of his father, Bert Lahr, gives the background of the little people quest, which began with Bill Grady, the casting director, approaching Leo Singer. Singer could promise only 150, so Grady sought out Doyle.

Doyle, who disliked Singer intensely, said he could easily line up the whole 350, but wouldn't if Singer had anything to do with it. Singer was told he was not needed, and Doyle did the job.

"The Major gets these midgets for me," Grady said. "They come from all over the world. Now I've got a date. I'm going to bring them out West in the buses. The meeting place was the Times Square Hotel on Forty-third Street. I had these buses pull up there. We were going to bring about one hundred and seventy midgets out of New York. . . .

"The first three buses are loaded. They are to go through the Holland Tunnel and on through Chicago. The first bus starts *up Broadway*. They are supposed to go down Eighth Avenue. . . .

"So I followed him. Leo Singer lived at Sixty-eighth Street and Central Park West, on the fifth floor. Major Doyle took the three buses and arrived at Central Park West. They waited at the curb in front of Singer's house.

Charlie Becker, left, with Freddie Retter and Carlo Santucci, a musician. (Courtesy of Janet Clemento)

(L. to R.) Chief Thomas Kennan, Major Doyle, Raymond Schultz.

"The major got out and went up to the doorman. 'Phone upstairs and tell Leo Singer to look out the window.'

"It took about ten minutes. Then Singer looked down from his fifth floor window. And there were all the midgets in those buses with their bare behinds sticking out the window."

Billy Barty, too young to have been one of the Munchkins, was asked if he had heard of the incident.

"No," he said, laughing, "but it could have happened. They were pretty wild in those days."

The incident became known as "Major Doyle's Revenge."

Leo Singer's Midgets certainly were one of the best-known groups. The troupe was formed in Vienna, before World War I, at the suggestion of Singer's wife, who had been an entertainer. A tiny city was built and became very popular as an attraction.

Their fame soon spread across Europe, and Singer's Midgets appeared in theaters in many countries. With the outbreak of

Elmer Spangler leading Singer band. Inset shows Spangler as master of ceremonies for musical-in-miniature. (Photo by Atwell, Chicago.)

Singer's Revue. (Atwell, Chicago.)

A scene featuring Lady Godiva.
(Atwell, Chicago.)

The oriental influence. (Atwell, Chicago.)

war, however, Singer moved his operations—and his little people—to the United States. After the war they returned to Europe, but only on tour. The United States had become their home.

Other groups came and went, but for many years Singer's company was the most famous and successful in the world. Doyle is said to have disliked Singer because the latter wouldn't hire him, and because he didn't treat his talent properly. Other sources say Singer, his wife, and Wally Singer, Leo's brother, were excellent employers.

Nonetheless, working under such circumstances, whether with Singer or lesser groups, surely created a feeling of dependency which must have prevented many of the little people of the era from acquiring the dignity and assurance that today's little persons display.

The Screen Actors Guild, for example, did not admit to membership until 1970 actors who also were little persons, although they had been permitted to work under a guild waiver for half a century. Billy Curtis, with more than fifty movie credits and numerous appearances as a stunt man, doubling for child actors, was the force behind the rule change.

"We've enjoyed many years of not paying dues," he said, "but my pride was hurt. It's like saying because you aren't five feet five you can't vote for President of the United States. I say we're not freaks. We're the same as big people. Maybe we can't reach the top shelf, but we can touch the floor faster than they can."

Herve Villechaize, the tiny figure who plays opposite Ricardo Montalban in television's *Fantasy Island*, and also has made a motion picture, Carl Reiner's *The One and Only*, with Henry (The Fonz) Winkler, had to wait years before he was "treated like everyone else."

The Paris-born Villechaize, who also is an artist and photographer, came to this country in 1960. He learned English by

Large photo, Rose's Midg
inhabitants of Morris Ges

...ing tribute to the Lone Eagle. Inset: a Parisian Follies, advertisement. To the left below, ...le Town, N.Y., Worlds Fair, 1939. To the right, Henry Kramer's Midget Starlets of 1942.

The Flora Dora Sextette, Midget Village, Century of Progress Exposition, Chicago.

watching television, and eventually drifted into acting, although he found it impossible to get such work in Paris. His first major break was as Knick-Knack in *The Man with the Golden Gun.*

Even after that, he was living a hand-to-mouth existence in Hollywood. He slept in cars, or moved in with friends and, as he readily admits, occasionally stole food to eat. In 1976, before the *Fantasy Island* role came his way, he was jobless and penniless.

When he was refused unemployment compensation, he wrote a letter to that office telling them they were responsible if he did anything "desperate." A check came at once.

Herve, who turned down other parts because he felt they were offered purely on the basis of size, is delighted with his role as Tattoo.

"I'm beginning to be recognized as an actor and not a circus act," he told one interviewer, Nancy Friselle.

What he means can be emphasized by quoting from some of the reviews of a 1938 motion picture, *The Terror of Tiny Town.* This film later was listed by Harry Medved, the young screen buff, in his book *The Fifty Worst Films of All Time.* The quotes:

"As all the cast are midgets, the element of surprise is lost and the film tends to be just another Western. . . . Everybody seems to be riding everywhere." (*Monthly Film Bulletin*)

"Quaint. . . . The hard-riding, two-gun boys go buckety-buck on Shetland ponies. The heroine escapes the villain by running under furniture instead of around it. . . . The formula drama has been given pint-sized treatment." (*Hollywood Reporter*)

"Contrived . . . doll-like personalities." (*Variety*)

Since then Curtis, one of the actors in *Tiny Town*, has had a number of good film parts. Michael Dunn, dead in 1973 at thirty-nine, won a nomination as Best Supporting Actor for his role in *Ship of Fools* in 1965. Barty, whose movie appearances now number more than 130, was touted by critic Pauline Kael for his work as the dwarf in *The Day of the Locust* in 1975. He also was highly praised when he played opposite Rod Steiger in *W. C. Fields and Me*, and in 1978 was cast as a sidekick of Jerry Lewis in a movie called *Hardly Working.*

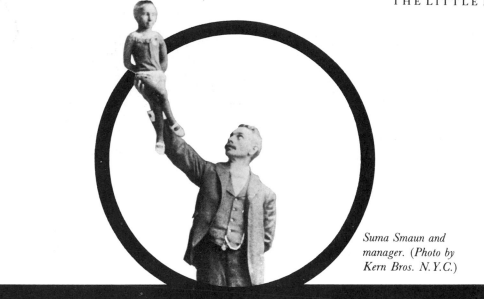

Suma Smaun and manager. (Photo by Kern Bros. N.Y.C.)

The Strange and Bizarre

THE LIFE OF CAROLINA Crachami, "the celebrated Sicilian Dwarf," provides one of the most poignant accounts of any member of that select company known as the little people.

She was the daughter of Louis Emanuel Crachami, a native of Messina, where he worked as a theater musician for many years before taking his family to Palermo. According to a brief pamphlet published in London in 1824, Crachami himself was 5 feet 5 inches tall and "well proportioned." His wife's height is not given, but she is described as being "justly considered a fine woman." There were three other children of normal stature.

When Carolina was born on November 15, 1814, in Palermo, it was immediately obvious that she was extremely small. However, several "medical professors" who examined her agreed that everything about her was so well proportioned that she probably would live to a "considerable" age.

Although the tiny lady was kept "very private" in Palermo, the Duchess of Pa-

lermo and other illustrious persons came to see her. Finally, through what means is not clear, Carolina was taken to England when she was something over nine years old by a certain Gilligan. There she was exhibited in Bond Street, presented to His Majesty, King George IV, and scrutinized once again by a panel of medics who confirmed that she was "the most perfect dwarf of which any authentic record is preserved."

The 19-inch 5-pound Carolina must have made quite a bit of money for Gilligan, and presumably for her father, who also was in London, because the unknown author of the fifteen-page pamphlet that covers all of Carolina's career mentions that "different branches of the Royal Family, and more than three hundred of the nobility, have been among the visitors of the last few days, and their testimony, in addition to that of nearly three thousand fashionables, is conclusive as to the unique form and interesting manners of Miss Crachami."

Then follow excerpts from news stories by writers who visited her. One of the bewitched journalists wrote in the *Literary Gazette:*

> Only imagine a creature about half as large as a new-born infant, perfect in all its parts and lineaments, uttering words in a strange and unearthly voice, understanding what you say, and replying to your questions . . . here is the fairy of your superstition in actual life; here is the pigmy of ancient mythology brought down to your own day. The expression of her countenance varies with whatever affects her mind (for on my faith, there is a mind and soul in this diminutive frame!) Her beautiful tiny hand (for the forefinger of which, the ring of a very small shirt button would be much too wide a round) has all the motions and graces which are found in the same member of a lovely woman; she laughs, she threatens, she displays her fondness for finery, she likes her drop of wine, she shows her pleasure, she chooses and rejects; in fine, she is as perfect as a common child of the same age."

Two weeks later, on May 15, 1824, the same writer again described a visit with "my fair friend Miss Crachami," who "sat upon a small tea-caddy with infinite grace, and listened to music with evident pleasure, beating time with her tiny foot, and waving her head just as any boarding-school Miss in her upper teens, and conscious of the beauty of her movements, would do. . . ."

Carolina must have been equally taken with the reporter, for she not only gave him a ring but permitted him to measure her. The results: height, 19½ inches; length of foot ("Cinderella was a nobody!"), 3⅛ inches; length of forefinger, 1⅞ inches; circumference of head, 12⅜ inches; waist, 11¼ inches; neck, 5⅜ inches; ankle, 3¼ inches; and wrist, 2 7/16 inches.

Lest you think the figures false, this is what the representative of the *New Times* wrote after his visit to the Bond Street levee:

> "Miss Crachami . . . is exceedingly well-formed; the hands remarkably good; knows a little English, and has a good ear for music. She has altogether the appearance of a genuine Lilliputian woman at her full growth, and is, we believe, the smallest of all persons mentioned in the records of littleness."

Whatever Miss Crachami's state of mind—happy, bored, impatient, passive—it didn't last long. The following month the London newspapers announced her death, one item stating:

> This poor child had been for some time afflicted with a cough . . . and the untoward changes in the weather . . . had a visible effect on the general state of her health. On Thursday last she was exhibited as usual, and received upwards of 200 visitors; towards the evening a languor appeared to come over her, and on her way from the exhibition room she expired.

Louis Crachami began searching for his daughter's body the next day, but was unable even to find Gilligan—for good reason. The miniature bed and the dress that was fashioned for her appearance at court were in the Duke Street apartment, but no clues to the dead child's whereabouts. After frantic inquiry Crachami discovered that Gilligan had sold the body—for a fee to be collected later—to the College of Surgeons. The bereft father rushed to that building, but arrived too late to prevent dissection. Gilligan, so far as is known, was never caught.

Carolina was not yet ten years old. Nor was she permitted privacy even after her death. When the surgeons were done with their explorations, the little skeleton was placed on exhibition at the college museum next to that of Charles Byrne, the Irish Giant.

Miss Crachami, certainly, was one of the most unusual little persons of all time, because of both her size and her symmetrical beauty. But there is no shortage of unusual little men and women.

Addie Eva Frank, born in New York City in 1890, weighed only 22 ounces at birth and fitted into a cigar box. But she lived to adulthood.

Jolly Bonita Gibbons.
(Wendt, N.Y.C.)

Hop, the Human Frog, a lively attraction in nineteenth and twentieth century circus and sideshow, was born in Fairfield, Iowa, in 1865 and grew to 18 inches and 30 pounds, although (so his billing went) lacking ribs, arms, backbone, and legs. Also known as Major Gantz (his real name was Samuel D. Parks), Hop took to show business after raising cattle for a number of years. He eventually married the Princess Wee Wee and owned his own show. He died in Long Beach, California, sometime in the twenties.

There are others: The Maharjah of Baroda's court jester had two wives. He was 30 inches tall, and they were two of the tallest women in the state.

Great Peter the Small could be placed in a top hat.

Pauline Musters, born in Holland in 1876 and dead of alcohol and pneumonia at twenty-two, was less than 22 inches tall and had been trained as an acrobat by her parents.

The Doll Lady, or Mademoiselle Coretta, who arrived in Clinton, Iowa, in 1890, was killed at the age of twenty-two when a horse, frightened by a windblown hat, reared and threw her out of a buggy.

Jacob Hoffbauer, one of the Singer's Midgets troupe, had two grave handicaps, in addition to being only 41 inches high. He was grossly overweight, and he had some defect in his balancing mechanism which meant that he had to be accompanied for fear of an accident in the bath or on the stairs. One night in 1931, apparently while trying to fix a radio aerial, he fell three floors from his hotel room and landed on a fire escape—but survived.

Then there was Lya Graf, a 21-inch performer with the Ringling Brothers Circus, who happened to be nearby when the financier J. P. Morgan was about to testify before the Senate Banking Committee in Washington, on June 1, 1933. The photographs of Miss Graf, seated on the sur-

Sideshow run by Hopp, the Human Frog, and wife Princess Wee Wee. Hopp was also known as Major Gantz. Insets show Gantz.

prised Morgan's knee, where she had been placed at the instigation of an enterprising photographer—who reportedly was not a Morgan fan—were seen around the world. Lya was famous.

But within a few years she had returned to her native Germany, now ruled by Hitler and his Nazis, and both Lya and her parents were sent to the death camp at Auschwitz. Many other little people also were murdered by order of fanatic Nazi officials. The hated Dr. Mengele reportedly staged a party at Treblinka—another of the dreaded camps—for a group of those he sent to the gas chambers the next day.

Not all little people were, or are, star-crossed, of course.

Anne Clowes, a native of England, died in Derbyshire in 1784—109 years after her

Prince Nicholi, posed as if he were Charlie McCarthy. (Circus World Museum, Baraboo, Wis.)

birth! And another Englishwoman, Mary Jones, lived for 100 years. Even Jolly Bonita Gibbons, who was born September 8, 1872, and eventually weighed 250 pounds—which looks like a lot more when it's distributed over a 42-inch-high frame—and Carrie Akers, a Virginia miss whose 35-inch body weighed 300 pounds, did not die young. Bonita lived into her sixties, and—judging by her photograph—Carrie Akers was still in show business with Barnum when she was at least forty or so.

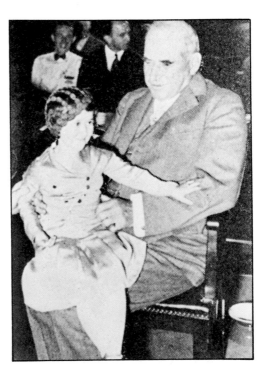

At top, Princess Victoria with own specially designed car. (Collection of Stuart Schneider.) Below, J. P. Morgan and Lya Graf. (Circus World Museum, Baraboo, Wis.)

Dickie Sorenson and his mother. (Circus World Museum, Baraboo, Wis.)

Giantess and little people, photographed at Baker's Art Gallery, Columbus, O., in 1893.

Little people of India posed with giant (1907).

Suma Smaun kisses a large lady. (Steve Balkin Coll.)

Love and Heartbreaks

FEW LITTLE PEOPLE HAVE had more interesting and fortunate lives than Joseph Boruwlaski, who was born in Russian Poland, near Chaliez, in 1739 and died in England ninety-eight years later. He was coddled by a countess, befriended by kings, and well known to scores of members of the nobility in several countries.

Boruwlaski was 8 inches long at birth, one of five sons and a daughter, of whom three of the boys were normal size, the other two, and the girl, miniature in stature. When the father died, Joseph was eight years old, and a friend of his mother, the Starostina de Caorlitz, offered to take the youngster into her home and see to his care and education. Mme. Boruwlaski accepted the offer because it seemed best for her son.

The Starostina, however, was married four years later and Boruwlaski found a new patroness, the Countess Humiecka, who took him to her estate at Rychty, and when he was about fifteen, let him accompany her on a tour of Germany and France. By this time he was 25 inches tall,

and very handsome, as the portrait in the Royal College of Surgeons indicates.

He also had a quick wit and a ready tongue. When presented to the Empress-Queen Maria Theresa in Vienna, the Queen picked him up and placed him on her lap, asking what in all Vienna he found most interesting.

"To see so little a man on the lap of so great a woman," was his courteous reply.

Pleased, the Queen noticed that he seemed to be gazing at a ring she was wearing, and asked whether he found it pretty. Again the perfect response:

"I beg Your Majesty's pardon, it is not the ring I am looking at, but the hand, which I beseech your permission to kiss."

He kissed her hand. She tried the ring on his finger, and finding it too large, called a young girl to her side, took a ring from the child's finger, and gave that to Boruwlaski. The girl was Marie Antoinette, later Queen of France.

The Countess and her small protégé then went on to Munich, and thence to Luneville, where the eighty-year-old Stanislaus, former King of Poland, lived in exile. He invited them to stay in the palace, which already housed his own favorite little person, Nicholas Ferry, known as Bebe, a couple of years younger and two or three inches taller than Boruwlaski, who now measured about 26 inches.

Bebe, who seems to have been rather simple-minded, nonetheless became very jealous when Stanislaus paid too much attention to the new arrival. So when by chance only the two small men were present in the King's chamber, Bebe grabbed his tinier rival and tried desperately to thrust him into the fireplace, where logs were blazing.

The startled Boruwlaski, taken by surprise, began struggling and shouting and the King and others came running to the rescue. Stanislaus, outraged by the attack, ordered Bebe beaten and told him he could never again enter the King's presence. Boruwlaski, however, generously interceded for his attacker. Bebe was thrashed, but permitted to regain his former position in the King's favor when he apologized to the Polish mini-man.

It may be best to give a brief outline of the short life of Bebe before returning to Boruwlaski's lengthy one.

Ferry also measured 8 inches at birth. Contemporary accounts say he was taken to church for baptism on a plate, and that his first cradle was a wooden shoe. Also, an early account insists, his mouth was so small he could not be breast-fed by his mother, but was suckled instead by a goat. He could speak a few words by the time he was eighteen months old, but did not walk until he was two. His first shoes were less than 2 inches long.

Nicholas was a sickly child, marked early by smallpox. He was poorly fed, because his parents were impoverished. He lacked an adequate education, although it is probable that he was incapable of learning much. When he was six years old, he was about 15 inches tall and weighed only 13 pounds. King Stanislaus learned of the boy and had him brought to court from his native town of Plaisne. The King gave him the pet name Bebe, and assigned instructors, but to no avail.

He could talk, but lacked reasoning power, and while he was given lessons both in music and dancing, learned neither. His attack on Boruwlaski was not the first instance of jealousy, however. It is said that when he saw the Princess of Talmond, one of his unsuccessful tutors, fondling a dog,

Commodore Nutt pretends to propose to Minnie Bump.

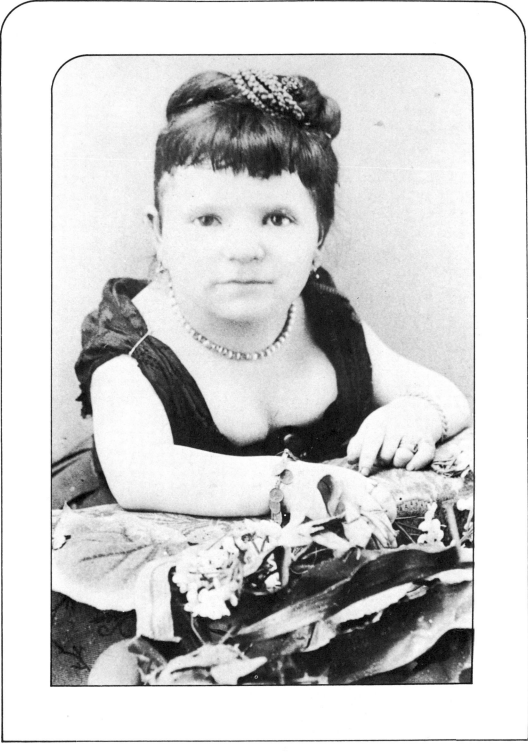

Henrietta Moritz poses for Eisenmann.

Above left: Suma Smaun and sister, Fatima. (Photo by Zwiefel, Dayton, O., 1910). To the right: Gen. Shade and wife (Sword Bros. Photo, York, Pa.) ·At bottom Count Magri and Jennie Quigley.

he seized the animal and threw it from the window, asking angrily:

"Why do you love her more than me?"

When he was twenty, Bebe fell in love with another little person, Anne Therese Souvray, to whom he was betrothed. But Bebe was failing fast. His backbone bent, his head dropped, one shoulder twisted, and his legs became weak, as his nose grew large. When he was twenty-two, he could walk only a short distance, and he died before he was twenty-three.

Mlle. Souvray took the name Mme Bebe. While the date of her demise is uncertain, she was still in show business in 1819, when she played the Theatre Comte at the age of seventy-three.

Stanislaus was saddened by the death of Bebe, whom he had buried in the church at Luneville, with an epitaph in Latin on the tomb.

Back now to Boruwlaski, who sometime during his long career acquired the "Count" in front of his name. When their visit to Stanislaus ended, the Countess and "Count" went to Paris, where they remained for more than a year. One of the highlights of their stay was a dinner, at which Boruwlaski was the guest of honor. Only small game and such tiny birds as ortolans and beccaficos were served, with plates and tableware made in miniature sizes, as were the knives, forks, and spoons.

Holland was the next stop after Paris. Then the wandering Countess and her little companion returned to Warsaw by way of Germany. As usual, wherever he went, the debonair Boruwlaski, an excellent conversationalist and fine dancer, was popular with the ladies.

Boruwlaski, now twenty-five years old, fell in love with an actress appearing with a French company in Warsaw. The woman, apparently amused by Boruwlaski's attentions, seems to have encouraged them while mocking her small suitor behind his back. At last he realized he was the butt of a cruel joke, and broke off the relationship. Meanwhile, the Countess had learned of the matter. After getting rid of a couple of servants who had helped Joseph in his intrigue, she temporarily withdrew her patronage. Soon, however, he was back in favor.

Not long after this Stanislaus II came to the Polish throne and graciously extended his protection to the little Count. When Boruwlaski was forty, however, the Countess took under her wing, as companion, a beautiful young lady, Isalina Barboutan, whose French parents were dwelling in Warsaw. Again the Count went head over heels—by now a 39-inch trip. Isalina was not even slightly interested, but when the Countess heard that Boruwlaski was enamored again, she first tried to reason with him, then had him locked in his apartment.

When he remained obdurate, the Countess angrily sent Isalina back to her parents and ordered Boruwlaski out of her house. This unexpected turn of fortune stunned Boruwlaski, who later noted in his memoirs: "The Countess Humiecka's bounty seemed likely for ever to secure me from want, and I did not foresee the probability of ever being deprived of her friendship."

He applied for help to Prince Casimir, brother of the King, and Stanislaus II promised to aid him. Meanwhile Boruwlaski kept wooing Isalina, who finally yielded. King Stanislaus gave royal approval, and also promised Boruwlaski an annuity of one hundred ducats. Six weeks or so after the marriage, Isalina told Joseph she was pregnant, and the Count realized that—despite the King's generosity—he was unable to support himself and his wife.

So Boruwlaski, after consulting with friends, decided to visit the many wealthy friends he had made during his earlier tour with the Countess Humiecka. King Stanislaus supplied a carriage and various letters recommending the couple to his royal confreres and the journey began on November 21, 1780. Boruwlaski was forty-one years old.

Isalina fell ill at Cracow, however, and the two remained there until her daughter was born. They reached Vienna February 11, 1781, just after the death of Boruwlaski's friend, Maria Theresa, but were aided by Prince Kaunitz, a longtime acquaintance. He also met Sir Robert Murray Keith, the British ambassador, who suggested the wisdom of a visit to England.

After a concert in Vienna, well attended by wealthy nobles and their ladies, the Boruwlaskis, who seem to have been on a kind of serendipitous journey, stopped briefly to visit some German courts, armed with letters from Kaunitz to his fellow princes. Then they traveled through various other countries, including Turkey, Russia, and Finland, before sailing for England from Ostend.

The four-day voyage was a rough one, and the ship lost her masts during a violent storm. But the reception in England made up for everything.

The Duke and Duchess of Devonshire befriended them immediately, finding them lodgings which the royal couple paid for. The Duke also paid for a suit, made by the Duke's own tailor, and introduced Boruwlaski and his wife to Lady Spencer, who presented them to the Prince of Wales.

Boruwlaski met King George III, and on the second such occasion, according to the wife of Charles Mathews, the English comedian, who also was present: ". . . the King rose from his chair and raising up Boruwlaski in his arms said: 'My dear old friend, how delighted I am to see you,' and then placed the little man on a sofa."

It's quite a jump in time from Boruwlaski to Elmer Spangler, who was the director of the orchestra of little people at the 1933 Century of Progress Exposition in Chicago. But they both had the same eye for the ladies.

Mrs. Doletta Boykin and her children standing in front of Tom Thumb's coach. (Century of Progress 1933.)

Mrs. Leslie, a fan dancer at Midget Village, 1933–34 Century of
Progress Exposition. Inset: Elmer Spangler.

Spangler, after romances with a couple of the unattached feminine residents of the Midget Village, fell hard for a fan dancer, the 4-foot 11-inch Rosalie, who seems to have been polite but not enthusiastic about his attentions. Spangler, who was 11 inches shorter, had trouble persuading her that he was serious. Until one evening . . .

Rosalie was dancing when someone fired a pistol. When the panic subsided, Spangler was discovered sitting near ringside with the gun in his hand. He was arrested and taken to court but the judge was sympathetic. Spangler explained that he simply had been trying to attract Rosalie's attention. The judge said the attempt would cost him five dollars.

The Marechal Midgets, Baroness Simon, Prince Dennison, Princess Marguerite. Rear, Marechal and wife.

Below from left to right: Mme. Shaw, husband, and daughter. (Photo by Strong and Root, Aledo, Ill.) George Townsend, son and wife; George and Ida Chesworth (Steve Balkin Coll., Photo by Empire, Los Angeles.)

Don Paco, the Spanish midget.

The Modern Little People

ODAY THERE IS AN IN-creasing interest in little people. The files of the two major Chicago newspapers—the *Tribune* and *Sun-Times*—contain photographic material and clippings about a great many such persons over the past forty years. Here, in chronological order, are the highlights:

1939—Thirty little persons from the Midget Village at Goldblatt's department store appear to ask Chicago immigration officials to extend their passports because their home countries are at war.

1939—The parents of the Del Rios—Trinidad, nineteen years old, 41 inches high; Paul, ten, 28 inches; Delores, twelve, 37 inches—are ordered in a Chicago court to pay $1,155 damages to a theatrical agent for violation of contract.

1941—Six small workers are used at the Brewster aeronautical plant, Newark, New Jersey, to crawl inside the wings of airplanes, where normal-size workmen can't reach.

1951—Survey shows how much more midgets pay for food, clothing, in comparison to what they get; also list of troubles and problems peculiar to the little person.

1953—Little Harvey of Hollywood, World's Smallest Cowboy, attends small persons convention in Des Moines, Iowa.

1957—First convention of newly formed Little People of America held in Reno. Riverside hotel gives free rooms, half-priced meals. Convention business includes demand for half-price fares on all public conveyances.

1959—Strategic Air Command base, Westover, Massachusetts, employs little person to crawl into air intake of F-104 Starfighter to remove any debris collected in flight.

1960—An eight-year-old girl found begging in streets of Taipei, Formosa, for funds to help ailing mother. Child is 2 feet 7 inches tall, weights 13 pounds 6 ounces.

1963—A 49-inch teacher instructs first-graders in Darrington, Washington.

Edna Mae Oliver and Singer's Midgets in 1920's. (Charles King Coll.)

1963—Photograph of LPA member unable to reach parking meter in Des Moines, Iowa.

1963—Dennis Binion, 3 feet 10, whose regular job is tax examiner for IRS, working as part-time elf, Atlanta shopping center.

1965—Daughter is born to English entertainer at Miami Beach. He is 4 feet 3, his wife 6 feet.

1965—The Marshall Space Flight Center, Huntsville, Alabama, uses 4-foot 7-inch expert to install electrical systems in *Saturn V* booster.

1966—Midget barber graduated from Cincinnati Barber College. He is nineteen years old, 4 feet 2, and uses a stand while working.

1966—Lee Kitchens, 4 feet 1, a developmental engineer, named LPA president during convention at Austin, Texas.

1967—Johns Hopkins study of thirteen below-normal-size youngsters indicates that psychological factors may have more importance in retarded growth than biological ones.

1970—Former "promotional mascot," 4 feet 3, now drives cab in St. Louis. He uses rope to pull trunk closed, and is known as Maxie the Taxi.

1972—Edmond Ansley, eighty-four years old, 4 feet 2, dies in Gainesville, Texas; he worked as a Buster Brown for twenty-two years.

1972—The 4-foot 5-inch director of publicity for Elmhurst (Illinois) College mentions a problem: "You have to get against the wall during rush hour to protect yourself. People literally are not aware of you and they can knock you down. It can be a frightening thing."

Ritter's Midgets.

Two candid photos of unidentified little people in zany show-type poses.

Prince Dennison.

1972—LPA convention held in Hillside, Illinois. Dr. Victor McCusick of Johns Hopkins, one of eight physicians attending, tells Joan Beck, *Chicago Tribune* reporter, there are "at least a dozen types of short stature represented among the Little People." The most common form of dwarfism is achondroplasia, in which the body is out of proportion.

1973—Mihaly Meszaros, professionally known as Michu, twenty-five years old, joins Ringling Brothers and Barnum & Bailey Circus in time for New York opening of season.

1973—More on Johns Hopkins study: "Deprivation dwarfism," caused by unhappy homelife, or possibly physical abuse, can be reversed if child is placed in happier environment.

1973—Night clerk at Sheraton-O'Hare Motor Hotel in Rosemont, Illinois, is 4 feet 6 inches tall. Hobbies are golf, baseball, hockey, and playing the clown for youngsters in hospitals.

1974—In answer to reader's query, *Chicago Daily News* column states that Manoel Souza, thirty-two years old, is world's smallest man at 2 feet 7 inches. (Michu is 2 feet 9.)

1976—Parnell St. Aubin, who was a Munchkin in *The Wizard of Oz*, runs a tavern called the Midget's Club on Chicago's southwest side, with wife, Mary Ellen, also small.

1976—The Short Stature Clinic at Los Angeles' Harbor General Hospital announces that study shows dwarfs, in general, are well adjusted "and have developed methods of putting [normal] people at ease and making them comfortable." Female dwarfs, however, were found to be better adjusted than male.

1978—A 3-foot 7-inch resident of Golden, Colorado, files complaint with Colorado Civil Rights Commission after being refused rental of an apartment because landlord allegedly told her she was an insurance risk because of her size.

Michu, the gregarious circus clown, was interviewed during a Chicago visit by *Daily News* writer Robert J. Herguth (now with the *Sun-Times*). Herguth (76 inches talking to 33) found Michu had an infectious sense of humor.

But he was worried about his weight, he told Herguth.

" 'I'm twenty-five pounds now, and I'd like to be twenty-two," said Michu, patting possibly the world's smallest incipient paunch. 'I like shrimp and fried chicken.'

" 'And you know, it's no cheaper for me to buy clothes than it is for you. I got this outfit in San Francisco. The shoes and jacket are all size 3, and my neck is a size 4.'

He told Herguth his foster brother, Tomi Liebel, also a clown, serves as his interpreter, and that his parents were members of the Lilliputian theater in Budapest. Michu added that he was satisfied with his size.

At top, Alva Evans, much-traveled circus clown. (Circus World Museum, Baraboo, Wis.)

" 'Big people have problems too,' he explained. 'Of course if I go someplace like a bar, there's trouble.'

" 'Trouble?'

" 'I can't reach the bar.' "

Before he headed for the ring, Michu imparted a bit of philosophy to his friendly interviewer:

" 'Life has many different corners,' he said. 'I see all the time from this corner. I can't do anything about it.'

" 'All life is a circus—yours, and mine.' "

The circus also has another of the world's best-known clowns, Prince Paul, who was born in Bangor, Maine, and moved to Boston when he was about six years old. His real name is Paul Alpert, and his three brothers and two sisters are of normal size.

Despite many efforts by his parents to aid his growth, nothing could be done. Even before he was graduated from high school in Roxbury, Massachusetts, Paul had begun appearing in vaudeville in local theaters with a friend in a song, dance, and comedy act.

"He used to carry me off stage in a laundry bag."

Prince Paul, as he was quickly named by one of the showmen, toured with small circuses during the summer, was bat boy and mascot for a semi-pro baseball team until a line drive almost hit him, and even demonstrated a metal polish in the window of a hardware store for the distributor.

"To this day I wonder what kind of chemicals he used," Paul said. "He used to say: 'Come on, shine it up again. Keep it silvery.' And this was about every two hours."

In 1935 a friend suggested that he send a résumé and photo of himself in costume to Ringling Bros., which he did. A contract came at once and he's been with that outfit since, except for time out during the war.

"When Pearl Harbor came I wanted to do something. But I was classified 004F, which meant I couldn't join the army or navy or anything. And I felt terrible. I wanted to do something for my country. So I went to the Red Cross and said I wanted to give blood. But the girl said: 'People have nine pints of blood, and you need the blood more than we do.' I felt terrible. She was very serious, so I went to the Boston Navy Yard."

There he was told he could become an arc welder, which he did after four or five weeks of instruction.

"I became very good at it. I'm still good. And I could read blueprints, too. I never thought the day would come when I could read blueprints. I did part of the work on the original atomic submarine, the *Nautilus*. I welded the protective shield. It was steel with a leaded lining, and I did the steel part. I made sure it was good. I didn't want any guys drowned."

He returned to the circus six months after the war.

Asked how he felt about the handicaps of size, Prince Paul laughed, which he does frequently.

"Those are the things you live with. You don't like it. It's irritating at times, but there are always ways of doing things. I've always said—a famous thing: I don't have any handicap. If there's a problem I go over it or under it or around it. I get around.

"I've never been bitter about being little, just angry. That made me overcome things. I never felt sorry for myself. I've helped a lot of people who had problems. They used to come to me for wisdom and—you know—encouragement."

Prince Paul never joined the Little People of America because after attending one meeting he was told there was a woman in the group who liked him and would be willing to marry him.

He never went back. "I didn't want to get married," he said.

In the off season he lives in Tampa, Florida, and spends his time visiting with friends or reading. He prefers adventures, a little romance, mystery, but demands good writing. And he concluded:

"There isn't a thing I've missed. I've had everything there is in life: love, traveling, good food, meeting people. In fact I think I've had better things out of life than most people. I'd say at least 80 percent better."

A small lady named Rosemary Pellicore was the recent subject of a two-page text-and-photo spread in the Arlington Heights (Illinois) *Sunday Herald*. She is 4 feet 2 inches tall—or, as Anna Madrzyk, who wrote the article, pointed out, "no taller than most of the six-year-olds she teaches."

Miss Pellicore has been a teacher for eight years and her current assignment is the Parkwood School in Hanover Park. When the reporter interviewed her it was in a first-grade classroom where Snow White and the Seven Dwarfs were displayed, which was "something of a breakthrough in her struggle to lead a full life in a world that often is hard on those who are different."

Miss Pellicore went into teaching because, while in a public school for handicapped children, she found others whose plight was worse than hers.

"She majored in education at Northern Illinois University in DeKalb. And it was at Northern, Miss Pellicore says, that she 'got myself together finally,' with the support of good friends and an active social life that included being social secretary for her dormitory."

She has found that her pupils are not curious about why she is small. None even has asked her about it. And if someone else says something, "they ignore it or give them a dirty look." Miss Pellicore lives in her own town house not far from the school, drives herself, and makes her own clothes. If she has something she can't do around the house, such as changing a ceiling light bulb, one of her colleagues drops by to help.

Hollywood gag shot. Man with hat is Don Tomalsky of Los Angeles.

Billy Barty, famous screen actor. Child photo shows him as leader of boy's orchestra. (Credit Arnold Mills Associates.)

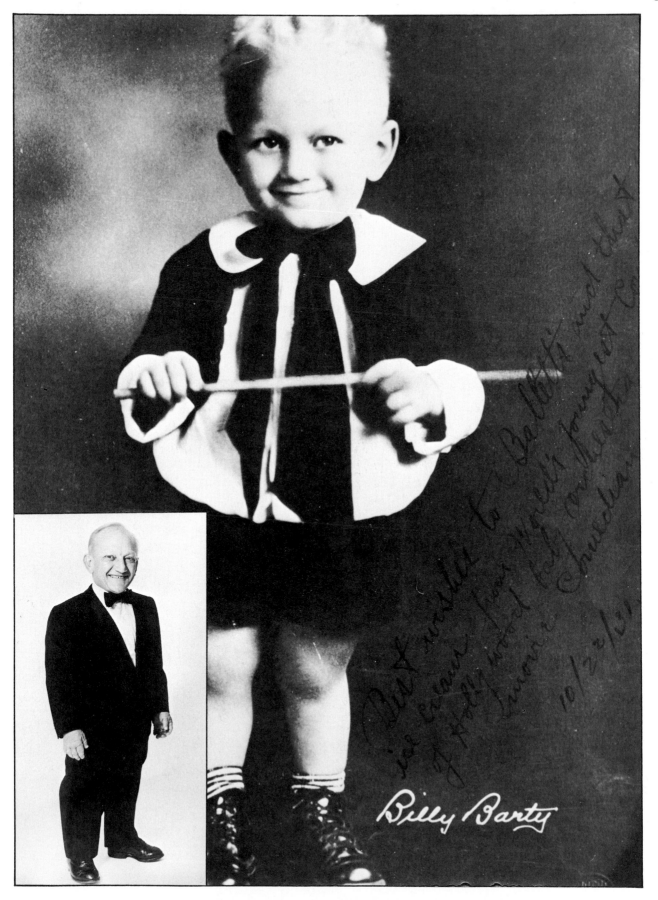

Billy Barty

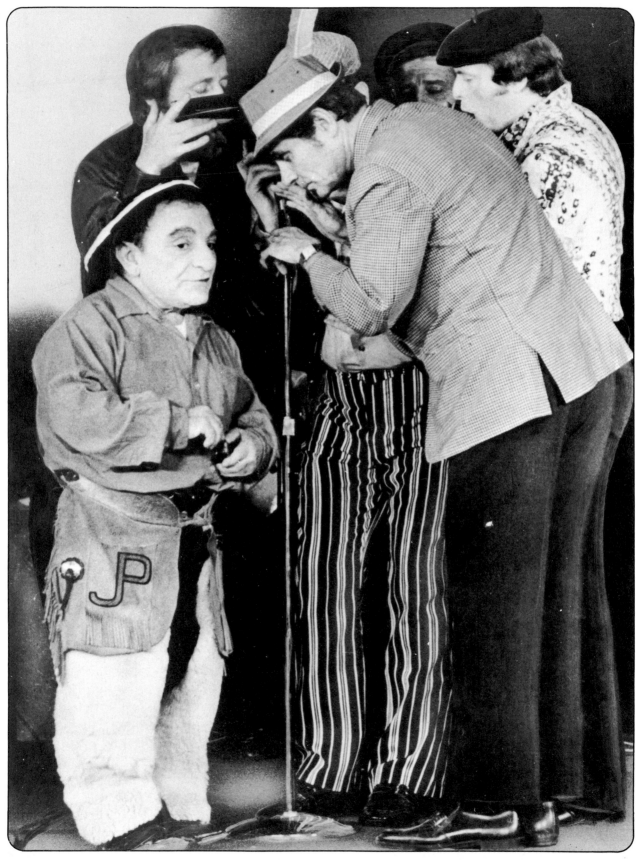

Johnny Puleo and harmonica gang, Blue Max Night club, 1972. (Courtesy The Chicago Tribune.)

She told Miss Madrzyk that she is considering joining the Little People of America, whose thesis is that there are two worlds to enjoy "and if you do away with the small one, you're really limiting yourself."

" 'I feel I have to find that other world, too. I want to know if others go through the same things. And before I die, I want to dance slow with a guy.

" 'People are too concerned about looks and appearances and I can't say I'm not either,' she said. 'But in a sense, you have to try to see the whole person. It's worth it.' "

Edward Darmstadt, seventy-four, lives in Oak Park, another Chicago suburb. He is a retired industrial chemist, a position he held for twenty years prior to his retirement in 1964 when his legs began bothering him. He is a former director of District 6 of the Little People of America and joined the organization in 1970.

"I wish I'd known about them long ago," he said. "I'd have been married by now." Darmstadt, who is 4 feet 7 inches tall—or three inches under the maximum allowed for LPA membership—drives his own car with the help of extension pedals.

He is wrapped up in the work of the LPA and never happier than when something good happens to a fellow member.

"One of our girls was working for a cleaning and drying establishment," he said, "and the owner's wife was picking on her, apparently resentful because her husband hired her. So she went to an employment agency and said: 'I will take anything.'

"They sent her to the Continental Illinois Bank one day, and she said the interviewer was a wonderful man, a gentleman, but that he showed a little hesitancy. So she said:

" 'Sir, I'd like to ask a little favor. Give me a chance, for one month.' She's still there, six years later. All we ask is that you *give* us a chance."

The group has a nationwide membership of 3,000, with the Illinois-Wisconsin enrollment about 300. Billy Barty, the national founder, says there are comparable organizations in many other countries: England, Australia, France, Germany, Holland, Sweden, New Zealand, Malaysia, Israel, and India. All have different names, but Barty's favorite is the English one: Association into Research of Restricted Growth.

The LPA was organized in Reno in 1957 with 20 persons attending. At the last convention, in Dallas, Texas, there were 542 in attendance. Headquarters, which may be shifted elsewhere, is at Owatonna, Minnesota, Box 126, Zip 55060.

Because of his status as an actor, Barty has had a great deal of publicity. He is 3 feet 9 inches tall, and weighs 70 pounds. He and his wife, Shirley, who is about six inches taller, have two children, Laurie, who is small, and a son, Braden, who seems on his way to normal height.

Barty was born in Millsboro, Pennsylvania, and shortly after he could walk was a part of his parents' vaudeville act. His first movie role was in *Wedded Blisters*, a two-reeler, and when he was five or six years old he was the leader of the Hollywood Baby Orchestra, about twenty youngsters who played, he says, "mostly violin and cello." He also was the kid brother to Mickey Rooney in about seventy-five of the Mickey McGuire comedy films.

In several interviews he has expressed the wish to do dramatic roles, but finds the supply suitable for little actors limited. In an effort to fill the void, he even has written a script for a projected television pilot with a lawyer (small of course) as the hero.

But let the headline writer for a feature story about Billy sum it up:

ACTOR BILLY BARTY:
A TINY PACKAGE HOLDS
A TOWERING TALENT.

Herve Villechaize with Ricardo Montalban from television series, "Fantasy Island" (ABC-TV) Inset: Herve charms pretty lady. (Courtesy of Columbia Pictures.) On left page, photo of Herve by Loretta Ayeroff.

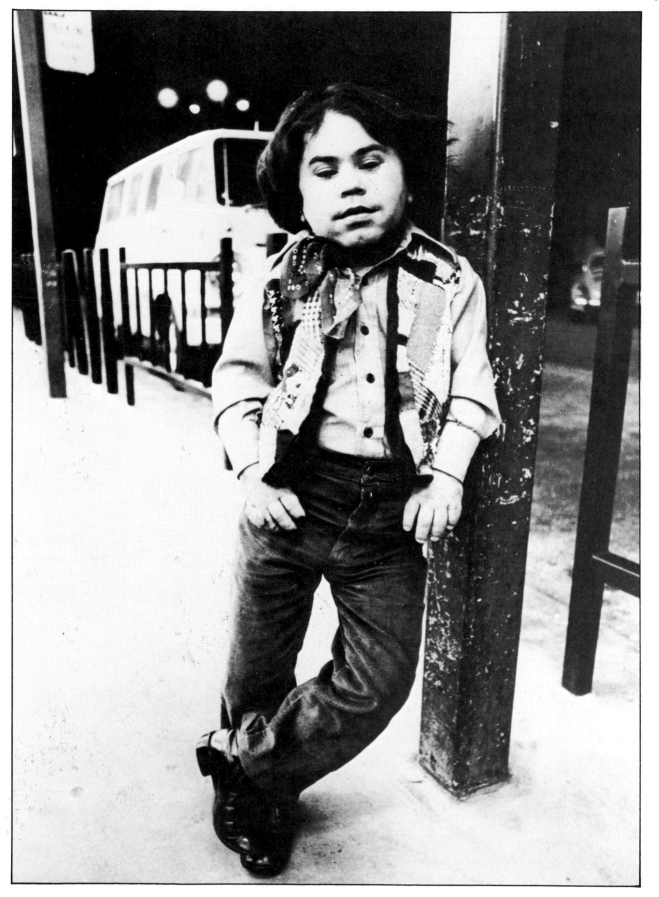

Wee Willie kicks Mighty Cupid, also leaps on him. Medinah Temple, Chicago, 1978. (Photos by Don Casper, courtesy The Chicago Tribune.)

"Leave 'em laughing," some wise man once said. So here's Eddie Darmstadt's most memorable experience:

He and another motorist arrived at a Chicago intersection simultaneously. Both stopped. Started. Stopped. The other man leaped from his car in a rage, calling on Eddie to step out and fight.

"I looked around and saw people on the corner," Eddie said, "and I figure he's not going to slug me in front of witnesses. So I got out and looked up at him. He just stood there, looking down at me, and his wife yelled at him from their car:

" 'Okay, big mouth! What are you gonna do now?' "

The man walked quickly back to his car and drove away.

Rosemary Pellicore, 4 feet 2, who teaches first grade in Hanover Park, Ill. (Photo courtesy of Arlington Heights, Ill. Sunday Herald.)

LPA meeting. Chicago 1978. (Courtesy, The Chicago Tribune.)

Bibliography

Atlick, Richard D. *The Shows of London*. Cambridge, Massachusetts: Belknap, 1978

Avi Yonah, Michael, and Shatzman, Israel. *Illustrated Encyclopedia of the Classical World*. Jerusalem Publishing Company, 1975

Barnum, P.T. *The Life of P.T. Barnum By Himself*. New York: Redfield, 1855

Benton, Joel. *Life of the Honorable P.T. Barnum*, Edgewood, 1891.

Brewer's Dictionary of Phrase and Fable, revised by John Freeman. New York: Harper & Row, 1963.

A Brief Memoir of Miss Crachami, Etc. London: Moncrieff, 1824

Bodin, Walter, and Hershey, Burnet. *The World of Midgets*. London: Jarrolds, 1935

Bowman, Harry P. *A Sunday Run*. Pennsylvania: Jeanette, 1942

Century of Progress Exposition. Chicago: R.R. Donnelley, 1933.

A Century of Progress Souvenir Book. Chicago: Regenstein, 1933

Chambers' Biographical Dictionary, Revised Edition. New York: St. Martin's, 1969

Clair, Colin. *Human Curiosities*. New York: Abelard-Schuman, 1968

Clarens, H.F. *Barnum and Bailey Route Book 1905 (A Brief History of the Circus)*

The Concise Oxford Dictionary of English Literature, Second Edition, revised by Dorothy Eagle. London: Oxford, 1970

de la Mare, Walter. *Memoirs of a Midget*. (Foreword by Carl Van Doren). Reader's Club Edition, 1941.

Dickens, Charles, *Sketches by "Boz."* London, 1836–37.

Dictionary of American Biography. Boston: James Osgood, 1876.

The Dictionary of National Biography. London: Oxford, 1960

Enciclopedia Della Spettacolo. Rome, 1958.

Encyclopaedia Britannica, Eleventh and Fourteenth Editions. Chicago.

Encyclopedia Italiana di Scienze Lettere ed Arte. Rome, 1884–88.

Fitzsimmons, Raymond. *Barnum in London*. New York: St. Martin's, 1970

Hammond, Harold Earl, ed. *Diary of a Union Lady 1861–1865*, New York: Funk & Wagnalls, 1962.

Lahr, John. *Notes on a Cowardly Lion*. New York: Alfred A. Knopf, 1969.

Lucas, E.V. *A Wanderer in London*, London: Macmillan, 1907.

Morris, Richard, ed. *Encyclopedia of American History*. New York: Harper & Row, 1976

McGlinchee, Claire. *The First Decade of the Boston Museum*. Boston: B. Humphries, 1940.

Official Guide Book, New York World's Fair, 1939.

Official World's Fair Weekly, Chicago, June 11, 1933.

The Oxford Companion to English Literature, Fourth Edition, edited by Sir Paul Harvey. London: Oxford, 1967.

The Pageant of America, Volume 14. New Haven: Yale University Press, 1929.

Plowden, Gene. *The Amazing Ringlings and Their Circus.* Caldwell, Idaho: Paxton Printers, 1968.

Root, Harvey W. *The Unknown Barnum.* New York: Harper Brothers, 1927.

Ross, Ishbel. *The President's Wife: Mary Todd Lincoln.* New York: Putnam, 1953.

"Sketch of Charles S. Stratton and His Wife, Etc." New York: Wynkoop * Hallenback, 1868.

Smith, Lady Eleanor. *British Circus Life.* London: Harrop, 1948.

Stirling, Edward. *Old Drury Lane, Etc.* London: Chatto & Windus, 1881.

Thompson, C.J.S. *The Mystery and Lore of Monsters.* London: Williams & Norgate, 1930.

Wallace, Irving. *The Fabulous Showman.* New York: Alfred A. Knopf, 1959.

Warren, J. Mason, M.D. "An Account of Two Remarkable Indian Dwarfs, Etc." Boston: *American Journal of Medical Sciences,* 1851.

"Wehman's Book on Giants and Dwarfs." Pamphlet by Henry J. Wehman, New York, 1890s.

Who Was Who In America. Historical Volume 1607–1896 (Marquis Who's Who, Chicago, 1963).

Wilson, Rufus Rockwell (commentary), *Lincoln in Caricature.* New York: Horizon, 1953

MAGAZINES, NEWSPAPERS, ETC.:
Bandwagon Magazine (article by John C. Kunzog, June 1953)
Harper's Weekly (1864)
The *Chicago Daily News*
The *Chicago Sun-Times*
The *Chicago Tribune*
The *Daily Herald* (Arlington, Illinois)
The Eclectic Magazine (1827)
The *New York Clipper* Magazine (1863)
White Tops Magazine (Rochelle, Illinois, 1946, article by Sverre O. Braathen)

Acknowledgements

FEW non-fiction books could be written without the assistance of a variety of generous persons. This one is no exception.

Our thanks are due first to Alfred A. Knopf, Inc. of New York for permission to use material from *Notes on a Cowardly Lion* by John Lahr; to Irving Wallace for his foreword; to Marilyn Roth for research; and Alice Cromie, who took time from her own writing to do much of the typing.

In addition, we wish to thank Bob Herguth of the *Chicago Sun-Times* for permission to use his story on Michu; Clayton Kirkpatrick, editor of the *Chicago Tribune,* for stories and photographs from that newspaper; Janice Lewis, reference librarian of the *Chicago Sun-Times;* and John Fischetti, the paper's political cartoonist; Ann Madrzyk, reporter for the Arlington Heights (Illinois) *Daily Herald,* for her story on Rose Pellicore, and the *Herald* for use of the accompanying photograph; Paul Kelvyn and Harry Trigg of WGN-TV for their help; and George Cohen, *Chicago Tribune,* for his.

Others whose aid was invaluable include Michelle and Clifford Krainek of Graphic Antiquity; Robert Parkinson and John Daniel Draper of the Circus World Museum, Baraboo, Wisconsin; Eddie Darmstadt, former Midwest director of the Little People of America; Billy Barty, founder of the LPA; Prince Paul, veteran Ringling Brothers, Barnum & Bailey clown, for an interview granted; J. W. Scheideman and other staff members of the Newberry Library; the Chicago Historical Society; Columbia Pictures; the Chicago Public Library; the Brown Shoe Company; Mickey Pallas of Chicago's Pallas Galleries; and the *St. Louis Post-Dispatch.*

The list is long, and perhaps unintentionally incomplete, but it must also include Archie Lieberman, the Evanston, Illinois photographer; Howard Whalen, actor and sculptor of Sierra Madre, California; Robert F. Looney of the Free Library of Philadelphia; another helpful researcher, Mrs. Sara Roth; Jack Nelson, Americana expert; Herve Villechaize, the *Fantasy Island* star, who was most generous; United Press International, and:

Mrs. Ralph Altman, Ken Apollo, Steve Balkin, Lurton Blassingame, our agent; Ron Becker, avid circus collector of Peoria, Illinois; Sanford Brokaw of the Brokaw Company; Joe Cavalier, Phil Chen, Janet Clemento, Marty Cohn, Charlotte Franklin, Jerry Gall, David P. Grath, Michael Greenbaum, Bob Hudovernik, Mr. and Mrs. Leon Jacobson, Charles King, Marvin Kreisman, Ellen Land-weber, John Lerch, Jack Levin, Jim Macatee, Victor Margolin, Arnie Mills and Associates, Matthews Weber Photos, Johnny (The Reb) McGuire, Frank Milligan, Al Niemic, Karin Perkins, Stuart Schneider, Charles Schultz, Bill Thompson, who edited the manuscript; Eldon Waldschmidt, Len Walle, Stanton Wanberg, Joe Weinberg, Ken Young, and—a special mention—Joel Kopp of America Hurrah Antiques in New York City.

Last on this roll call—a position we hope his White Sox never will find themselves in—ʟ the unmatchable Bill Veeck, who devoted a couple of hours of precious time to remembering Eddie Gaedel and one of baseball's most unforgettable moments.

We are grateful to them all.

THE AUTHORS